DANCING
WITH
POWER

Magic, Meaning and Mystery
in Everyday Life

FRANCIS D. NATALI, PHD

To my Dear friend
Thorne
and our good memories
Fran

Published by RavenSpeaks Press

P.O. Box 1870

Port Townsend, WA 98368

Cover Photography by Erica Natali
Design by D. Doreen Snyder

Printed in the United States of America

Dancing With Power; Magic, Meaning, Mystery in Everyday Life /Francis D. Natali; 1. Self Help 2. Spiritual

ISBN 0-9705041-0-1

∽ *Dedication* ∾

for Erica and Rico

Acknowledgments

I have come to believe that "personal" transformation is a team effort. I have been fortunate in having many wonderful people in my life who are both teammates and teachers. I thank them all. Unfortunately, there is only space to mention a few by name.

Chris Evatt devoted a large amount of her personal time to encourage me, coach me, and edit this manuscript at a time when she was busy with her own writing project. Her generosity is both inspiring and humbling. Liz Reutlinger and Baila Dworsky also volunteered time to read, edit and comment on the manuscript. I am very grateful for their support. My thanks to Doreen Snyder for her help, including the book and cover design.

My children, Erica and Enrico, continue to help me grow into a larger experience of the world. Their mother, Linda, has helped me to become a better parent (and person) with her example of compassion and courage.

My brother, Enrico, and his wife, Nadia, have been constant companions and guides in the process of learning to practice what is preached.

Dr. Jim Spilker, Jr., a friend and mentor who for over 30 years, has found ways to use my technical abilities while allowing me the freedom to explore life. Without him, my family would have been on much shorter rations. Dr. John Olson and Dr. Tim Cox put heart into a work environment where it was sometimes in short supply.

Bob Cowgill and Richard Hoskins have provided inspiration for over thirty years. Jim Tolpin and Ernie Baird pick me up when I fall down. Kit Africa keeps me laughing. Miguel Winterburn always challenges me to live more fully. Dominic Harper showers me with care.

I have been blessed with a "dream team" of fellow travelers and dance partners in Jackie Jackson, Jenno Schuller, Baila Dworsky, Liz Reutlinger, and Rainie Kaiton. Lisa Flores and Alison Hero are co-conspirators on the path.

So many more people that make my life rich come to mind. I hope they will accept my gratitude and do not mind remaining anonymous.

∼ *Table of Contents* ∼

Table of Contents

IN THE
BEGINNING

Go to Hell,

And stay there!

Or face

Your worst fear.

Rico's poem
Age 9

From a troubled sleep I crashed through a wall of wakefulness into a state of pure terror. Alarm bells were going off in my head and my body was experiencing uncontrollable spasms. I watched disks of light from cars on the busy street outside chase each other across the walls of my dingy motel room. I threw back the sweat soaked sheets and tried to get a grip. "First things first. Where am I?" I could not remember. There had been too many motels for too many years in too many places.

Events slowly began to organize themselves in my head. I was in Santa Cruz and it was Friday night. I hovered on the edge of the abyss of terror, fighting not to panic. If I could hang on until morning, I could get on a plane and go home where I would be taken care of . . .

I had grown up the son of an immigrant in a small town in upstate New York where we were isolated from main stream America. I knew little about the outside world–I don't remember ever eating in a restaurant, going into a barbershop (my father cut my hair), or owning a suit until I graduated from high school.

At the age of seventeen I left home for college. I had been accepted at a private engineering institute with a reputation that attracted students from the upper social strata, many of who had attended prep school. Harris tweed jackets, striped ties, button down shirts, and madras Bermuda shorts were the standard apparel that signaled class membership–a Princeton haircut was a must.

My roommate told me later that, on the first day, he had to make a quick decision whether to request a room change or to attempt a complete remake of the character in front of him. He and the other guys in the dorm generously decided on the remake. It wasn't long before I looked "collegiate".

I was always gregarious and functioned well in the everyday world, but the society that I discovered left me with a deep sense of bewilderment.

Everyone seemed to agree on what success and 'the good life' were, and how to go about achieving them except me. I couldn't understand why people lived the way they did, but I assumed they knew something I didn't and was too timid to let on that I didn't "get it." So, I tried to live like everybody else.

I did well in college and received undergraduate and graduate degrees in Electrical Engineering. I then began to pursue an engineering career in earnest. While I was good at my work, I didn't enjoy it. My interest in technology, discovered when I became a radio amateur at the age of twelve, died a natural death when I was about eighteen. Unfortunately, I felt that the die was cast and continued on a path that held no real interest for me.

I had married my college girlfriend at the age of twenty-two, even though I no longer had any interest in her. Once again, I felt I had to do what other people expected of me. The disastrous relationship ended in divorce seven years later.

When I turned thirty, I began to consider how I might live my life differently. At thirty-four I married for the second time and within a month had resigned from my job with one month's notice. Linda, my new wife, and I were determined to live in our pick-up camper for at least a year (we had saved the elegant sum of $3000 to finance this trip).

Two weeks later Linda informed me that she was pregnant, and I withdrew my resignation.

Five years passed before I tried it again. This time I informed my boss—and mentor—that I was quitting to move north and become a carpenter. He, being a man of some understanding, replied, "You don't have to quit. Just go north and be a carpenter. You can work for us when you feel like it."

The move to totally new surroundings had a big impact on both my wife and me. Linda blossomed in the new environment. She made friends and found a new confidence in herself. I, on the other hand, felt lost and isolated. My assessment of my woodworking skills was that I was good at making sawdust but not much else. I felt incompetent and useless—my self-confidence eroded rapidly.

The inevitable happened. Problems in our marriage that had seemed manageable suddenly were insurmountable. My wife decided to end the marriage. I was crushed by this turn of events. The pain and turmoil of the following months were occasionally interrupted by moments of insight that renewed my interest in life, but these moments were rare and I had little will to go forward.

At the age of 40 I was having a classic mid-life crisis. It was a crisis of the mind that questioned all aspects of my life but didn't produce any answers. A year later, my wildest dreams came true when Linda had a change of heart and we were reunited.

In the meantime I had met a cabinetmaker who, after a trial period, suggested that we become partners. The reality of building kitchen cabinets in a cavernous, drafty, unheated barn, (with a cement floor) in the winter was not terribly romantic or exciting. The temperature held between 30 and 40 degrees and the short days were generally overcast.

We worked at an unrelenting pace with marginal equipment in unsafe conditions (we quit early the day the planer blades shattered and threw shrapnel all over the shop). The stress was worse than my professional job and, with our income averaging about $5 an hour (and sometimes less), engineering began to look pretty good.

A second child after the marriage reconciliation, along with the decision for Linda to stay home while the kids were young, required that I have a steady income. Inevitably, part-time engineering became a way of life. Every few weeks I would fly to California and work for two or three weeks in the high-tech electronics world of Silicon Valley. The management of our growing company bent over backwards to accommodate my unusual life style.

My mentor, who was one of the company founders, showed unlimited faith in me. He would often call me to work when a job was in trouble. I became very good at

dealing with these difficult situations and was romanti-
cized by my colleagues as a gunslinger who rode into town
to set things right. The popular conception was that in
between saving electronic damsels in distress, I lived the
rugged life of a woodsman at home in nature.

In truth, my life felt schizophrenic. At work the environment was both tense and intense. I lived in motels (I
usually picked cheap ones to save the company money) or
with friends for several weeks at a time. I became a
connoisseur of motel art, a subject worth a book all by
itself. I existed in a constant state of guilt, first because of
my involvement in the defense industry (which I often
felt bordered on the criminal) and secondly because I was
away from my family so much of the time.

More and more my time at home was spent recuperating
just so I could leave and do it all over again. Nonetheless,
I felt that I was doing what was necessary as a husband
and father. However, as with most coping strategies, what
seemed to be working was not.

And then it happened, that Friday night in Santa Cruz
when the middle-of-the-night terrors struck, and I woke
with heart bounding to battle demons while praying for
daylight. I don't know what physiological term would be
used to describe my condition that night—my guess is that
I was on the verge of a "nervous breakdown", whatever
that is—but it got my attention, and I didn't want it to
happen again.

When I returned home, I sat on the rocky beaches and
walked in the woods contemplating my situation. Did I
have the courage to face my own life? Would I quit my

job if I had to? Where would the money come from?
The questions kept parading across my mind like the
messages across an electronic signboard.

On the second day the confusion cleared and I was filled
with a sense of determination. Then I did what I usually
do at such times–I fell back on my Catholic tradition and
talked to whatever was out there running the show.

"I am not a slave, and I'm not dead yet. I'm willing to do
whatever it takes to have a life that makes sense, but I'm
tired of trying to figure it out. You tell me and I'll do it,
otherwise leave me alone."

Then I added, "Further, I am willing to be of service if it
is appropriate. I have been taking for almost fifty years,
and now I am willing to give something back if that is
useful."

The last statement was naive on my part, and I now
believe it was overkill. I had no idea the power those
words would unleash in my life nor the traumatic events
that would be set in motion to help me move forward.

Within two hours I was getting messages from the Universe, and my life began to change in an almost magical
way. One of the messages was not to quit my job but to
just proceed and my job would change. (This turned out
to be the case. I now work only on commercial projects).

One night, as I was commuting to California by train, I
woke up with a start at about 2 AM in my sleeper com-
partment. An inner voice urged me to get pen and paper
out of my briefcase and start writing. I complied and
began to write about the role of desire in our lives, the
paradox of desiring to be without desire, and how the

energy of the paradox can be used to move towards a greater experience of life (see Chapter 8, "Desire Demoted").

The process of writing was so strange as to be almost frightening. I felt as if I was "receiving" a message as opposed to writing from inside myself, as would be the case when writing a technical report or paper (something with which I was very familiar). I could follow the literal meaning of the "message" but didn't know if it really made sense.

To add to this feeling of strangeness, while I loved to read, I never had any interest in writing. I considered the writers I knew to be "word people" and a breed apart from myself. Nonetheless, the writing became a part of my life when I traveled.

I would often write at night or sitting by the ocean on weekends. Writing became my companion, and I seldom felt lonely. The nature of the process changed and took on the characteristics of a true partnership. The words were neither outside me nor inside me. They were not someone else's nor were they mine. They just were.

I was very surprised to see the words continue to string themselves together into a book-length manuscript. At home my woodworking tools lay idle while I spent more and more of my time typing what I had written in longhand while on the road. This process continued for almost two years before I felt that it was complete.

The manuscript indicated there was a different way to operate in this life than the one I knew. It suggested that one could change from a self-centered creature to a "centered-self" from which "appropriate action" would arise. And one would live in harmony with the unfolding Universe.

While I recognized the merit of the message, it seemed absolutely unobtainable for a person such as me. Also, it seemed like too much work to attempt a path that required discipline I neither had nor desired. After all, I already had one brother that had become a Jesuit priest and another that had carried on an intense Zen practice for the last twenty years. That was enough for one family. I didn't want to be serious like my brothers. I wanted my life to get easier not harder, and I wasn't really interested in changing myself. I just wanted my life to change!

However, subtle changes had been occurring over the past two years. I now seemed to have an open line of communication with something larger than myself, so when I declared, "I think I get the point of this material, but I couldn't become the person it describes. I could fake it, but I couldn't be it", the voice in my head replied: "That's right, this is material you could teach, but you're not ready to teach it".

If I had been smarter, I might have seen what was coming and begged for mercy.

After finishing the manuscript, I left for a brief stint at work in California and returned about a week later. My wife met me at the airport, which was unusual. Her sister was taking care of the kids so we could spend the night in the city. I was tense and out of sorts from the trip and was certainly not much fun to be with. However, I sensed an underlying tension that went beyond my own condition. What was meant to be a wonderful time ended by being awkward and disappointing.

A couple of days later my wife said, "I can't do this anymore. I want a separation."

My world collapsed. I felt like a drowning man who is overwhelmed by a raging sea. My crying, begging, and pleading only drove a deeper wedge between us. I tried every trick in the book to get her to change her mind. I continually returned to the theme of "How could you do this to our kids?" certain that the guilt would wear her down. Our daughter was 15 at the time and our son, Rico, was only six.

At one point I said, "This is not fair to Rico and me."
"This is not about fair", she replied.
In retrospect, this is one of the most profound statements I have ever heard.

In my panic, I turned to the inner voices and confronted them with, "How could this happen. What's going on? I'm doing everything that you told me to do."
"Here's your chance to learn this stuff", a relaxed voice replied.
"Wow, you guys play hardball!"
"Hey, this is not your worst fear come true. It's only your second worst fear."
I could feel the prickling of goose bumps as I spread my hands in a gesture of compliance and said, "Okay, we'll do it your way—let's go."
My worst fear was that one of the kids would die.

That was ten years ago. The time has passed quickly, and yet it seems like lifetimes. When I felt most sorry for myself, friends who had read the manuscript would say, "Hey, you ought to read your own book!" I have certainly been given ample opportunity to practice what is preached, although I have come to think I am a slow learner.

I recently reread the manuscript after not looking at it for some time. My first reaction was to laugh out loud. It struck me that the unseen power that surrounds us had had itself some fun at my expense.

The book makes the path of "appropriate action" and "completeness-in-the-moment" sound easy. I had no idea what the consequences of committing to this path would be nor how painful it would be for me to change. I am sure I would not have had the courage to proceed if I had known.

During one particularly dark time in the process, I sat mourning a lost love (a woman I had dated for several months). My heart was breaking and in my self-pity I pleaded, "Why do I have to loose her? Will this pain never end?" Immediately I heard a very clear inner voice saying, "Do you want her? You can have her right now, and this process will stop. We thought you wanted what you asked for—to live a meaningful life that makes sense." I couldn't believe what I was hearing, but my response was immediate: "No, I've come too far to turn back now. This and more—whatever it takes, go for it!"

On the one hand I'm amazed that I have survived the pain of change to this point, and on the other hand I can't imagine being the person I used to be. The pain of change is dwarfed by the pain of a life without meaning. The underlying theme of my life, which has always been resistance and struggle, has had to change—my approach to life has undergone a complete revolution.

My life, which had been built on quicksand, is being

rebuilt on solid ground. Everyday living, which used to seem incredibly complex, now seems simpler. There is a sense of flowing instead of resisting. Weak relationships have not survived. My indulgent habits and self-centered actions appear to be under constant attack. I am, out of necessity, becoming a stronger person.

It occurred to me recently that this book is not about creating what you most want in life or even about feeling good all of the time, although it gives some insight into these matters. Rather, it is about coming alive–which I think is the heart of the matter.

I don't believe that I could or would write this manuscript the same way now. However, it still rings true for me, and my experience has given meaning to much of what I didn't understand. My journey continues. I am passing the manuscript on to you in the form that it was given to me. I hope that it serves you well.

There was once a man who lived in front of a mirror. He was fascinated by the reflected images and became obsessed with gazing at them. He was totally enamored with the daily goings-on of the mirror world in which, it is probably no coincidence, he played a central role. As time passed, he grew convinced that the images were real, and he began to forget there was anything outside of the mirror.

One day, through an event as mysterious as life itself, he found himself behind the mirror looking at its back, which was all black. Since he had long ago forgotten he was looking into a mirror which had a back, he perceived that his world had become a black abyss and was terrified. In that moment of panic, something inside of him came unstuck.

Sometimes now, he would find himself in front of the mirror, but the reflected images didn't seem quite as real as they once had. Other times, he would be looking into the blackness of the back of the mirror, but the blackness wasn't quite so terrifying. In rare moments he would not be looking toward the mirror at all.

THE
MANUSCRIPT

⋙ *Introduction* ⋘

We live in an "Age of Reason" in which the mysteries of high technology have, for the most part, blinded us to the mysteries of life. The miracle of one hundred thousand transistors on a wafer of silicon smaller than a dime seems more interesting and exciting than a blade of grass or a leaf from a tree. We all strive to hone our technical skills and children become acquainted with computers at an early age. Our role in the creation of the semiconductor chip gives a pride of ownership that is lacking in birds and wild flowers.

Unfortunately, as we turn away from reverence for nature in our fascination with the wonders of technology, we threaten our own existence. Pollution, deforestation, and ozone layer depletion cause us serious concern. At the same time, we can't imagine living without our cars, TV's, and dishwashers. It seems that civilization is headed toward disaster with no way to turn back, so we race forward with no viable alternative—but hope for something to save us. Many of us long for participation with a deeper sense of meaning but don't know what to do or where to look for direction.

Science, on the one hand, offers us an impersonal Universe that is, at the fundamental subatomic level, run by chance. Religious leaders, on the other hand, threaten us with a Universe that is so personal it takes offense at the slightest indiscretion and can be vengeful beyond belief.

Caught in the middle and frustrated, you may choose to be self-reliant and look deeply at the nature of your own life. This situation is not unique to our time. People have, especially in the East, been seeking self-realization and enlightenment for centuries. However, the unique conditions of our society call for unique approaches that make the mystery surrounding us accessible.

If all of the passengers run to one side of a boat, there may be danger of capsizing–our situation is not much different. We have rushed to the "rational" side of the boat and the "mystical" side looks woefully empty. However, if we all rush for the "mystical" side things will not be any better. The path to self-realization is a balanced integration of the mystical, rational, and physical realms. In this way we can come into harmony with our surroundings and ourselves. I believe the approach described here is a step in that direction.

Life is an ever-changing mystery that unfolds in and around us. We are faced with an infinite variety of forms and events whose underlying purpose remains hidden to most. The only thing that seems to be certain is that nothing is certain. The only constant is change.

Humans have been searching for the "meaning" of life for thousands of years. We are continually trying to satisfy some inner need that remains elusive. In the midst of this confusion there is at least one underlying characteristic of life that is consistent. Life, it seems, is a learning experience. We are repeatedly faced with situations that provide us with the opportunity to learn new things and broaden our awareness of the mysteries around us. Not all of these opportunities are pleasant, and life is often considered to be a "school of hard knocks".

We occasionally hear of people who seem to have stepped off the treadmill of the ordinary man. They act with an assurance and sense of knowing that is beyond our experience–in their presence one senses something solid and at peace.

These people are from a diverse group, and most of us are inspired by at least one of them, past or present. It might be Florence Nightingale, Mother Theresa, Ghandi, the Mahareeshi, a Zen master, a Hopi elder, a martial arts master, a metaphysical adept, Krishnamurti, or any number of other inspirational presence's. These people hold out the hope that each of us can discover the key to a life of purposeful fulfillment that is free of the burden of anguish.

Often the example set by these people appears as inaccessible to us as if they lived on the moon. Their lives seem to have no relation to the work-a-day world in which most of us exist.

Can we discover the same sense of fulfillment, power, and peace in our everyday lives as these extraordinary people exhibit in theirs? I assume so–each of us is, after all, as much an expression of the human experience and the uniqueness of the Universe as any other being on the planet. If one can do it, so can others.

Since the cloisters, Zen monasteries, ashrams, martial arts dojos, and Native American sweat lodges are not for most of us, we must find fulfillment amidst the chaos of the modern world. Many people are living this challenge, and I believe with some success. The challenge I am talking about is to go from a life where something is missing, undone, or stagnant, to a life in which you know that you are doing exactly the right thing at the right time and everything is in its proper place. That is, to change from a life of searching for happiness with only rare moments of experiencing true joy, to a life where everything "makes sense" and is permeated by feelings of "unreasonable joy," appreciation, and fulfillment.

A colleague told me that the high point of his life was to stand at the helm of a large sailboat with a strong wind blowing. The power of the wind was awesome and being in harmony with that power was an incomparable experience. The dance that unfolded between the wind and the boat was one of great beauty. To experience this same feeling every moment is one description of the transformed life.

There is a saying that, "A good sailor always sails downwind and never misses his landfall". How can we always sail "with the wind" and still get where we are going?

The wind of creation blows through the Universe. If we are alert, we can feel it in our lives. By aligning ourselves properly, we can move forward effortlessly and in harmony with this force of nature.

Do I know that such a force really exists and that a life assisted by, and in harmony with, this force is possible? Well, history and experience are on my side. Lao Tzu set forth the fundamentals of Taoism some 2300 years ago in the Tao Te Ching. The ancient Chinese philosophers saw the Universe as structured by the Tao. Within the Tao is energy or chi. This is the energy that supports the world of polarities known as yin and yang. The Universe is in continual transformation flowing between yin and yang. Christians have a different view but also recognize an unseen force, which they experience as the "Holy Spirit" or the "presence of Christ". In fact, most cultures believe in a force (or forces) which permeates the world and affects our lives. I choose to simply call it "power". This is the power that can transform lives without really changing anything.

The invisible wind of creation is felt by all of us, but not all are alert enough to sense its presence and direction. I assume that this is by design, but who knows why? Not everyone is ready to harness this power. After all, as you learn about this power, you make yourself available to it. Sailing a boat in a strong wind is a tricky business, and one must learn the fundamentals. This is also true when using the power of the creative force. We seem to be so well protected from the full force that it is inherently difficult to proceed too rapidly (with a few exceptions such as the use of hallucinogenic drugs or extremely intensive unguided meditation). In fact, it usually takes a firm commitment to make enough progress to satisfy us, and the "seeker" often experiences much frustration. Frustration, however, is just part of the journey, and once you've started, it is difficult to turn back.

We are spurred on in our search for fulfillment by talk about Enlightened Masters. We also have the example of Christ who appears to have been a master of "appropriate action" and a living embodiment of love. Buddha extends to us the promise that we are all Buddha. Is this a cosmic joke designed to make us look foolish when we fail to attain the impossible? Should we attempt what may be an unachievable goal? In one way, we have no choice. Birth launches us on a search for fulfillment, and we seek until we find it or die.

Personal transformation is coming into harmony with the forces of the Universe, so that one experiences the exhilaration and beauty of life without anguish. You become like a hawk on the wind, not free of the wind, but employing it to soar effortlessly. Is this a metaphor for achieving fame and riches? Perhaps–but not necessarily. Fulfillment lies in different places for different people.

In church I heard the story of a young monk who saw St. Francis of Asissi hoeing in the garden. The monk approached and asked respectfully, "Tell me Father, what would you do if you knew that you were going to die tomorrow?"

"Finish hoeing the garden," St. Francis replied. This is an example of a harmonious life.

⇌ *Before You Begin* ⇐

To assist you in understanding the concepts in Dancing with Power, I have written concise definitions of the main ideas in this book. Read these now and refer back to them if the terms seem vague or confusing.

COMPLETENESS IN-THE-MOMENT
Each moment is complete in itself. That is, everything you need for fulfillment is present each instant. The quest is to experience this completeness.

RESOLVE
Make a firm decision to experience completeness-in-the-moment (which may also be described as fulfillment, enlightenment, oneness, universal love, total appreciation, or just joy-without reason). Be committed to this goal and pursue it relentlessly.

THE MESSENGER
Feelings of anguish or suffering are signs that you are resisting the flow of life. View this discomfort as a "messenger" sent to tell you that it is time to let go of comfortable beliefs and judgments. Be willing to move into the unknown.

LEARNING THROUGH DISASTER
Many people would rather live in pain than heed the messenger of internal anguish. They fear letting go of the known. The typical person creates disastrous situations until he or she hits bottom or dies. It is better to respond to the messenger's call and step willingly into the unknown.

DISCIPLINE
Prepare for the unknown by developing courage, daring, and attention through mental and physical discipline. The key elements of discipline are meditation, physical exercise, a healthy diet, dropping judgment and self-image, and letting go of chaos. Seek a clear mind, healthy body, and loving heart.

POWER
Resolve and discipline bring you in contact with "miraculous power." Practice focusing this power which can turn your visions into reality. Enlist power as an ally to assist you along the path to completeness-in-the-moment.

CLEAR MIND
Learn to make a distinction between "thinking mind" (logical, analytical) and "silent mind" (intuitive, inspirational). Neither aspect of the mind should dominate. Bring these two parts into harmonious balance through

discipline. Strive for a "clear mind" in which "silent mind" reveals appropriate action and "thinking mind" implements it.

GUIDANCE
Power is useless in achieving fulfillment without the wisdom to use it appropriately. Seek "guidance" by surrendering to a knowledge that is deeper and more fundamental than that of "thinking mind." Become alert for clues and trust your intuition implicitly.

APPROPRIATE ACTION
Assume there is an action (or inaction) appropriate to each moment. Trust guidance to reveal this path and then act without expectation.

RESPONSIBILITY
Take responsibility for your life by considering each situation a gift and an opportunity for greater learning. Never perceive yourself as a victim. Act without regret and embrace the consequences of your actions whole-heartedly.

IMPECCABILITY
Proceed on the path of appropriate action as though you had no doubts, even though you understand that the Universe is unfathomable and your assumptions and beliefs may be false. Strong resolve, a courageous heart, natural discipline, and total responsibility epitomize an impeccable life.

APPRECIATION
Appreciate the gift of life exactly as it is given—embrace it

joyously. Make your life a living example of appreciation and gratitude.

MASTERY
Master yourself and you will become a master in any situation. If you are complete, without need, and do not ask the world to be different than it is, suffering will cease.

SERVICE
As you become complete and without need, you will see life's dramas clearly–and you will know what needs to be done. Having nothing pending, you may choose to render service.

DANCE WITH POWER
Know when to push forward, when to give way, and when to sit and wait. Resolve to experience completeness-in-the-moment. Call upon guidance to show the way. When action is appropriate–act. If impossible coincidences are required, call upon the power of the Universe to support you. Become attuned to the energies of nature and sense their ebb and flow. Conduct your life in harmony with these energies and you will move forward effortlessly–dancing with power.

part 1

MESSAGES

Conquer your fear with stride,

Look at yourself with pride.

If you are afraid of hunger,

Go hungry.

If you are afraid of sound,

Listen!

Erica's Dream
Age 12

The material presented here is like a bulletin board plastered with messages for different people. Walk up to the board and scan it, looking for messages addressed to you. Unfortunately, some vandal with a childish sense of humor has blacked out all of the addressee names, so you can't tell which messages are yours! There is no way to judge each message as right or wrong without the context.

Since you don't know whom it's for, read each message without judgment. As you read these messages ask, "Is this message for me?"

The messages hint at the beauty of the most common surroundings, the mystery of the most common occurrences, and the possibility of a life without internal conflict. You may think that you recognize certain messages as being for you, but you can't be sure. If you decide to act on any of them, do it as though your belief is a certainty and proceed with complete confidence.

≋ 1 ⁀

THE ZEN
OF LIFE

Philosophy is thought, Zen is experience.

A farmer in medieval Japan was reputed to be enlightened. One day, a Zen monk, seeing the farmer approaching with a sack of grain slung over his shoulder, called out, "What is Zen?"

The farmer put down his burden and stood silently.

The monk, after realizing that this was his answer, asked, "Ah yes, but what is Zen in action?" The farmer shouldered his sack of grain and resumed his journey.

If the Zen of life is life in action, why must we seek profound answers?

One morning, I had coffee with a woman who has been a spiritual seeker for many years. Her path was seldom easy and was, at times, burdensome.

"Sometimes," she commented, "the striving for enlightenment becomes too much for me. All I want to do is sit here watching the steam rising from my coffee and smell the wonderful aroma." Suddenly she smiled and said, "That's it, isn't it?"

We have all heard stories about spiritual seekers who meditate for years, yet the point is made again and again that living in the moment is the ultimate goal. This is epitomized by the reply a Zen master gave to the question, "What is Zen?"

"When you are hungry eat; when you are tired sleep."

Life in a Zen monastery is strictly regimented. A friend, Jeff, who had lived in one, told me about a novice who continually disobeyed the rules and often napped during work time and snacked between meals. When the Zen master asked him why he engaged in such behavior he replied, "When I'm hungry, I eat, and when tired, I sleep".

The Master promptly kicked him out.

In odd moments this story would come to mind, and I would wonder about the Zen Master's harsh response. After all, the student had responded appropriately. Several years later the answer occurred to me–the novice was a lying dolt. He ate when he wasn't truly hungry and slept when he wasn't really tired! He lead a slovenly life of half-truths and weak actions. The Zen master was not angry, he understood that the novice was not ready for the rigorous discipline required for monastery life.

What is the difference between a Zen master eating and a typical man eating?

Attention.

The Zen master has become a master of attention and

focuses on the moment. Since he pays attention, his actions are appropriate to the situation and are not born of habit. He does not eat just because it is lunchtime; he only eats if he is hungry. And when he eats, he truly experiences eating!

Likewise, he does not lie down to sleep out of boredom; he sleeps when he is tired and awakens rested.

But so what? He meditated for years so he could pay attention when he eats...why? The answer is enjoyment. Have you ever noticed how eating is more enjoyable when you are truly hungry? Yet many of us eat out of habit more often than hunger. Most people talk or even read while eating, often with music playing in the background. In this chaotic state, the experience of the moment is lost.

The ordinary man lives in a state of distraction rather than attention, and without attention there is no true fulfillment.

≋ 2 ≋

D I R E C T
E X P E R I E N C E

The past is dead, the future a dream.

Life is a mystery that unfolds moment by moment. The only experience we can have is in the present instant. Thinking of things past or things future, our experience is still limited to the present moment. Most of our experience is the "indirect" experience of thinking about the world with very little direct experience of the world in the moment.

For example, I am lying quietly in bed and it is raining outside. The falling rain makes sounds I can hear; if I look out of the window I see the rain falling. If I walk out of the door I feel the rain on my skin. In this moment I have the opportunity to experience the miracle of rain directly.

Instead, I have been thinking that I must get moving—it is going to be a busy day at work. I hear the rain and after a reaction against "bad" weather, I think about how slow traffic is going to be. I anticipate getting wet with distaste, and when I go out the door, I run to the car to minimize my exposure. Once in the car, I mull over the possibilities of catching a cold from being wet. A battle ensues between the "positive thinking" and "realist" factions within me about the physical and mental causes of colds. This has been my experience of the miracle of rain.

No wonder I have feelings of something undone or missing in my life! I crave direct experience but don't allow myself to have it. One of the most difficult things to do is the simple task of experiencing the moment directly. The thing I crave doesn't require money, physical stamina, or good looks; it only requires attention. I have looked for fulfillment in status at work, a closet full of clothes, a meaningful relationship. In the past I have accepted any number of defeats rather than look where the problem lies.

A drunk is crawling around under the street lamp looking for his pocket watch. A Good Samaritan passerby helps in the unsuccessful search for some time before expressing his surprise that they haven't been able to find the watch. The drunk replies that he is not surprised, since he didn't drop it here anyway. The passerby exclaims indignantly, "Then why are we looking here?"

"Because this is where the light is!" replies the drunk.

Likewise we continue to look for fulfillment where it is easiest to look, but where there is no hope of finding it. True fulfillment can only be found when we begin to pay attention to the present moment in our lives.

Does this mean there is no such thing as meaningful work or meaningful relationships that can give us a sense of fulfillment? No, it only means that nothing can be fulfilling unless you pay attention to it in the present moment. Further, as you become able to pay attention to every moment, everything you do becomes fulfilling.

There are many ways to "shock" ourselves into experiencing the moment directly. One simple and effective technique for achieving a direct experience of the world is to hit your thumb very hard with a hammer. (I have done this, by accident, and I experienced the pain very directly. I wasn't worrying about what the boss thought of my latest memo or the high price of gasoline when my thumb was swollen and throbbing).

So what? Am I going to keep hitting my thumb to waken myself to life? It doesn't sound like a very good recipe for discovering the miracle of the moment. However, for some people, the craving for direct experience overrides the distastefulness of pain and so they create pain in their lives.

Self-torture has been an important part of religious practice through the ages. St. Francis of Assisi prayed for, and received, the Stigmata (the wounds of Christ). They are reported to have been very painful with continual festering and open sores. You can imagine that this was a powerful reminder for St. Francis to experience Christ in everything that he did.

The Sun Dance of the Plains Indians (which is still being practiced today) requires, among other things, that the participants pass thongs through the pierced skin of their chests. The thongs are tied to a tall pole set into the ground. The dancing continues until the thongs pull through the skin, often taking a day or more. The excruciating pain totally eradicates the chatter of "Thinking Mind". This non-thinking state often allows the participants to receive very powerful spiritual insights.

However, just as the forest returns to life after the noise of the hunter's gun subsides, so does the mind slowly return to its ceaseless chatter when the pain stops. Pain stills the mind only temporarily—and since self-inflicted pain can lead to obsession and morbidity, it is best avoided.

Another simple technique for achieving direct experience is physical fear. Most people have had a very close call in an automobile. The instant you realize that you are in grave danger you are drawn into the present.

Once again, this technique is often used to satisfy the craving for direct experience of the here and now. Take, for example, the proliferation of pastimes such as skydiving, hang-gliding, bungy cord jumping, white-water canoeing, and a host of others. Such comments as, "I never feel so alive and free as when I'm doing this," are commonplace.

Fear, however, can only provide brief moments of satisfaction and so is not helpful in developing continued attention to the present moment.

There are other simple techniques, such as sexual orgasm and strenuous physical exertion that can be used to engender direct experience, but they also provide only a very temporary solution.

Many people come upon a teacher; one who lives in the present and helps to bring them to the same state of attention. There are thousands of monasteries, zendos, and ashrams where many thousands of people are drawn to meditate and experience the world directly. But there are still millions of people with this inner need waiting to hear the same message in a way that is meaningful to them.

This brings us to another alternative, which is the discipline of attention in everyday living. I prefer this path because it can be practiced at any time, in any situation. However, it is difficult because it is so subtle. Without ceremony or trappings to make a process "special", it is hard to change our old habits.

To proceed, you must first understand what you are looking for. Your experiences of pain, fear, sexual release, and physical endurance are invaluable to you, since they familiarize you with your quarry. Once direct experience is recognized, you realize you can create the same state by merely willing your attention to the present moment. Unfortunately, the experience is extremely fleeting at first— the running internal dialog quickly obscures the experience.

With practice, the experience can be sustained for slightly longer periods of time. At this stage, you begin to notice that Thinking Mind depends on such artifices as judgments, desires, and other commentaries on the external world to sustain its running dialog. You determine to drop judgment and desire. As you are able to achieve this through self-discipline, the mind becomes quieter because it has less fodder to chew.

Now you come to a crucial realization. The mind's chatter depends on discussing, describing, and judging an external world that is separate from you. You then attempt the ultimate maneuver, which is to drop this view of separation between yourself and the world around you. If you are successful, the mind no longer has anything to chatter about and only direct experience of the moment is left.

Wisdom is not born in Thinking Mind. Wisdom is universal and is tapped when the internal dialog has stopped. Thus those who allow internal silence become wise, and since direct experience brings joy, they become joyful.

≈ 3 ≈

FEELING
COMPLETE

In the world of the fox, nothing is missing.

Humans are seekers because life seldom feels complete. There is a feeling that something is missing, a yearning for a fullness that isn't there. But what is missing?

Could it be money? When we get more money, we seem to need more. Is love the answer? We've all loved and been loved, and it didn't seem to solve the problem or make us feel complete for long. Relationships aren't It. Maybe the accumulation of material goods is the answer. Nope. Wrong again.

As children we didn't want to go to bed until our parents did. We were afraid we would miss something; grown-ups have all the fun. As grownups we still suspect that others are having more fun than we are, and if we could just be in their shoes, our problems would be solved—we would get the brass ring.

As my friend Jim, standing on the beach for a moment before returning to work, commented, "What a beautiful day! Wouldn't it be great to be somebody else so we could enjoy it?" As great as it might be, we are stuck with who we are so let's proceed.

As we pursue each experience in search of completeness, we succeed only in finding where the answer is not.

As old age approaches we have an unpleasant realization: There are too many places where completeness may be hidden and time is running out. So we stop. We feel defeated. But must we? Not necessarily—let's review our position.

We have tried to feel complete in many ways, but whatever we try fails. Freedom from inner disquiet is illusive—or temporary at best. All our actions have been based on the belief: To feel complete, we need something more than we already have. Let us consider a different point of view:

Everything we need to feel complete is available to us right now.

If this is true, why don't we know it?

Have you ever known a child who, to be the center of attention, continually asks for things he doesn't need or really want? If his parents indulge his every whim, does he stop asking?

Of course not. The more he gets, the more he wants. his neediness is entirely manufactured. It gives him control over the situation, which is what he really wants.

Is it possible that, like a spoiled child, our neediness is entirely fabricated?

Consider your Thinking Mind as a spoiled child who is out of control. It distracts and disrupts you with its demands so it can run the show. So what is the alternative? To quit attempting to placate your Thinking Mind by meeting its impossible demands and restore proper balance to your awareness.

The first step towards resolution is to recognize that all attempts to resolve inner need by looking to the external world are doomed to failure. This is because the solution does not lie out there. The solution is to achieve an integrated awareness in which Thinking Mind plays a balanced and harmonious role.

"But how can I achieve such a balance?"
First, you must desire to be free, to no longer be tyrannized by Thinking Mind. The next step is to observe your Thinking Mind's behavior in an unbiased manner. This can be done through meditation or by witnessing your mind's antics in daily life. Once you have become adept at observing your Thinking Mind, you can begin to quiet inappropriate responses. As this happens, a much more subtle knowing occurs. Appropriate action will begin to occur out of an intuitive awareness.

With appropriate action comes attention to the moment as though a veil has been drawn from before your eyes, and a sense of completeness will begin to predominate. These are the first signs of a balanced awareness.

THINKING MIND

The first thing to remember about thoughts is that they are not reality.

Reality, whatever it is, is not resident in our thinking. This may seem obvious, but the truth is that we believe our thoughts represent the real world. In fact, we each walk around with our own "story". Everyone has a story. Think of it, six billion different stories walking around on the Earth, each convinced it is the one and only true (and by far the most important) story.

We honestly believe our story reflects the way "it" really is! This is the "world of illusion" referred to by sages from time immemorial.

I used to think an enlightened person would see things with an entirely different form since he or she would see through the illusion of the everyday world. I now believe an enlightened person sees exactly what I see—but from outside their story.

My brother, Enrico, says, "We are like tape recorders, each

with his own tape playing. Whatever is on the tape we take to be reality. If we perceive something is wrong with the tape recorder, we try to fix it by changing the tape." Good luck! The whole tape recorder must be functioning properly in order to play the tape—there is no way that changing the tape will fix the tape recorder.

In Enrico's analogy, the material on the tape is seen as the content of consciousness while the tape recorder is consciousness itself. And while our thinking may arise out of a conscious reality, it is neither conscious of that reality nor can it change it.

Consider the role of Thinking Mind. Does the Master who has achieved "Empty Mind" still think? Of course! Empty Mind coexists with Thinking Mind, but thought does not cloud experience. Thinking Mind is used as a tool to enhance rather than block out life. It is a very important part of our being and should be disciplined, trained, and utilized.

The difficulty comes when we believe we are our Thinking Mind rather than Thinking Mind being part of the whole. Believing we are our Thinking Mind is a viewpoint that lacks balance and this imbalance is reflected in our lives. We become slaves to rational thought and lose our intuitive connection to the situations that life presents.

Indeed, you must think to do a mathematical computation or to prepare dinner. But—what if you start thinking about the mathematical computation while you are preparing dinner? Your attention wavers, your dinner burns, your math is faulty.

But is concentration the only thing we are after? No, we

must take another step—a more difficult step. That is to achieve no thought when no thought is required.

If thought dies when it is not necessary, we can then experience peace. Having dropped continual chatter, the mind is no longer obsessed with fear and judgments. Now, when Thinking Mind is called upon, it is clear and strong. If you need to solve a problem, the mind is not distracted. If you wish to do historical research, the mind is rested and ready. If you need to formulate a plan for accomplishing a certain goal, the mind is bold and confident.

True knowing does not come from thinking about things but from dropping thought and being available to inspiration. Power points a direction. Thinking Mind assists in following the direction.

$\approx 5 \approx$

APPRECIATING
THE ORDINARY

Appreciation provides the energy for transformation.

At the age of 17, I spent two months in a hospital—I had
lung surgery, with subsequent complications. During my
convalescence, I spent many hours sitting by the window,
observing life on the street. The hospital was located in a
ghetto area of Chicago, and the streets teemed with
people going about the business of their daily lives.
At the time, I did not know if I would ever walk out into
the world again to share in its delights. The freedom to
cross a street seemed like a glorious adventure, fraught
with possibilities. I understood then that life was a gift
beyond imagining, and promised: "If I am allowed to live,
I will become a living expression of appreciation and
gratitude for the gift of life." I vowed to pay attention to
life's magic and never say, "I'm bored."

I often think back on these promises. There are so many
things in the world to find fault with—pollution, commute

traffic, nuclear arsenals, war, taxes, and one's inescapable death. But when I criticize what exists, am I showing appreciation for the gift of life? If Aunt Martha gives me a tie for Christmas, and I complain about the big red polka dots, am I being appreciative? Wouldn't it be better to embrace Aunt Martha and the tie, polka dots and all?

True appreciation is embracing everything as it is. Value judgments have no place in this scheme of things.

One of my first "teachers" was a boy whom I met in the hospital.

A nurse took me to a floor below mine to visit a twelve-year-old boy who had been in an iron lung since the age of eight. I didn't know if he was totally paralyzed but could see that he was totally enclosed in a steel cylinder, except for his head. As I got better, I visited the boy frequently.

When I walked into the room, his whole face glowed. A visitor was a glorious gift and he showed total apprecia-tion. He was always cheerful and never complained, but much more than that, he was serene–he had no business deals cooking, no place to go, nothing pending. I had his total attention, and he welcomed me without reservation. I always left wondering, "How can someone with so little give so much? "

I am often amused by how difficult it is for me, with all I have, to be appreciative. His was an example of true appreciation in action.

One evening, I discussed appreciation with my friends, Jim and Carl. Jim embraced the idea of appreciating everything but Carl didn't.

"You're not being realistic. You are denying the evils of

the world," said Carl fervidly. "When I took my walk this morning, I had to cross a bridge with a polluted stream under it. Then I saw aluminum beer cans and plastic picnic trash on the beach. After work, I drove home in rush hour traffic. How can I condone this? I feel terrible, not for myself–because I'm old and won't be here much longer–but for my kids and grandkids who must live in this mess."

Jim had no response and the friends parted.

A week later, Jim called Carl, who sensed that something was bothering him.

"You sound terrible. What's wrong?"

"After our conversation I decided I would adopt your attitude. I see the world as it really is and it is a mess. I see the ills and condemn them all."

"Hey, don't get depressed," Carl said, feeling guilty.

"What I called to find out is–does it work? Does condemning evil make it go away? Have you noticed any improvement where you are?"

There was silence.

I have found that judging situations as "bad" does not improve the quality of life. Only action can do that. Appreciating the gift of life requires seeing the world as it really is–and embracing all of it. This stance is not passive.

Work for change as you are moved to do so, all the while delighting in the world exactly as it is.

6

LETTING
GO OF
JUDGMENTS

The joy is in being the creator, not the critic.

Suspending value judgment is one of the single most powerful acts a person can perform to transform his or her life. We have been taught what is right and wrong, good and bad, from the day we were born. We are attached to our opinions and believe that we can tell the guys with the white hats from those with the black hats. Unfortunately, this rigid world-view exacts a high price, and we pay it unknowingly. Here's an example of how it works...

Ted, a co-worker, told me he had a strong dislike for homosexuals. Every time he saw a gay person on the street, which in San Francisco happens frequently, he was deeply offended. Then something happened. After changing jobs, Ted developed a close working relationship with Peter, his new manager. Soon the relationship blossomed into a wonderful friendship. One day, when Peter was absent from work, a colleague asked, "Do you know that Peter is gay?"

The news shocked Ted and forced him to re-examine his beliefs and feelings about homosexuals. He dreaded confronting Peter when he returned to work.

Two days later when Ted saw Peter again, he rushed up to him and impulsively embraced him. He decided his old ideas about homosexuals no longer had a place in his life and he dropped them. In his mind, homosexuals became "people"–not enemies. They no longer offended him–he had dropped the burden of judgment.

Judging what "is" is both fruitless and arrogant. All things that "are" are necessary to complete the whole of what is.

Suppose you are successful in suspending judgment. Does this mean you condone the nuclear arms race? No, it simply means you see the arms race as it is, something that simply exists, neither good nor bad–but very dangerous.

If you see a rape in progress, having suspended judgment would you ignore it? Of course not. Engage in action that is appropriate to the moment. It may, out of necessity, be violent.

Can we take action without making a judgment? Can a wrong be righted without it being called a "wrong?" Can violent action be taken without righteous anger? When I asked these questions of a Vietnamese martial artist, he replied:

"A martial artist trains for years to remain master of himself in any situation. If he is successful, anger and frustration do not hamper him, and his actions are precise and powerful. You may be very good and anger might still arise. In this case it never touches you–it is just energy and you direct it.

I doubt that anger arises in a true master."

The master takes complete responsibility for his actions and lets wisdom be his guide. As appropriate action arises, it manifests itself through him. He is a lethal opponent.

Every negative judgment you make is like putting a stone in a sack that you carry on your back. As judgments pile up, each step in life becomes a struggle. As you judge others, you also judge yourself and are drawn into continual conflict. The judge becomes the judged.

Connie, a friend, has meditated daily for the last ten years. Her particular meditative practice is taught by a guru in India who has many disciples. The meditation is specifically designed to enable the meditant to levitate.

One evening while Connie and I were having dinner in a restaurant, she confided that she was discouraged. "When I started the meditation program, I thought I would be flying around the room in a few months. It has been ten years and I haven't gotten off the ground yet. Other disciples are also discouraged, and one person filed a law suit against the guru because the program is very expensive."

"Why do you want to levitate?" I asked.

"To help bring about world peace and achieve personal enlightenment".

The connection between these things and levitation baffled me. I asked her to explain more.

"We believe that peace and enlightenment will happen when enough people learn to levitate. This idea is based on the ancient Vedic Sutra that says, 'When the yogi flies, the darkness of the world will be destroyed.'"

The power and beauty of the sutra overwhelmed me. I was overcome with euphoria and found myself saying, " You mean—when the yogi stops creating the darkness in his world, he will be free to fly."

The events and conditions of the world are what they are. The "goodness" or "badness" can only exist in our minds. We create our own dark view of the world through judgments, which become our reality. We are prisoners within our own dark creation, and only we can free ourselves from it.

During W.W.II, the killing of Germans was considered "good" by many people and was rewarded with medals and promotions. Of course, if you were a German mother, the killing of your son was "bad" and the killers were "evil". The killing occurred and the mind of the observer made it "good" or "evil".

Indeed, the "evil of the world" is a point of view. While we don't all agree on which events are evil, most of us agree we are surrounded by them. The fear, anger, and frustration resulting from this view are hardly conducive to the light and weightless feeling required for flight.

Darkness and evil are the judgments of the thinking mind caught in its never-ending struggle with duality. If Connie's meditation causes her to drop all judgment and experience the unity of the Universe, she will fly. If we all joined her, there could be world peace.

7

THE
MESSENGER'S
KNOCK

Beliefs are our shield against the unknown

My father once said to me, "Nobody is satisfied with what they have, but everybody is satisfied with what they know". This often seems to be true. We have our opinions and look about us for confirmation. We go to great lengths to rationalize our views rather than learn from the world and change as necessary. We'd rather fight than switch.

Our beliefs constitute a model of the world that allows us to understand our surroundings. Unfortunately, our model is just that and is no substitute for the real thing. The world we live in is unfathomable and can be experienced but not known.

We cling tightly to our model of the world because it is known. The unknown is frightening to us, so we hold on to our belief system to feel comfortable. This makes us rigid entities who are not served well in our fluid environment. To feel comfortable, we resist changing our beliefs even when the world presents us with object lessons that are contrary to our views.

Think of your view of the world as a room in which you live. It may be a small, unattractive room where you exist in poverty and pain, but at least you know every inch of it. Outside your room is the great unknown, and you don't want to go out there!

You understand why a man, who is unexpectedly paroled after serving fifty years in prison, is likely to commit a crime so he can return to prison. The pain of incarceration is less frightening than the world outside.

At some point, you may be ready to take a step toward expanding your awareness—or comfort zone. In response, the Universe sends a messenger. He knocks at the door of your small room. You ignore the knock. But he is persistent and calls for you to come out.

"There's no one here but us mice", you respond timidly, hoping humor will dissuade him. No such luck—the messenger bangs on the window.

"We don't want any. Absolutely no solicitors!" you yell while lowering the shades.

To your dismay, the messenger is not diverted and warns you that he will use force. When you don't respond, there is a loud crash as the door is broken down. You are dragged kicking and screaming out the doorway and find yourself in a larger, more attractive room with pleasant surroundings. You can enjoy the room until the messenger knocks again.

We are often so resistant to change that it takes a disaster to get our attention.

We then attract disaster so we may move to greater awareness.

My friend, Len, attended college on a football scholarship and expected to have a successful professional football career ahead of him. In his senior year, he had an automobile accident that broke his back and left him paralyzed. He spent several months in a full body cast. His doctor was honest with him and told him that he might never walk again.

"Don't worry", Len replied, "nobody is going to have to take care of me. As soon as I can move my arms, I'm going to commit suicide."

A psychologist was assigned to work with him in accepting his disability as well as the physical pain. Len, with the help of the psychologist, began to see the challenges and possibilities of being alive. Today he is completely recovered and works in behavioral psychology.

He told me that the automobile accident was the best thing that ever happened to him. "Before the accident nobody was good enough for me. I had no feelings and was as good as dead. Today I am able to be of service, and life is exciting and interesting beyond my wildest dreams!"

Most of us have had some traumatic event in our lives. As we think back on that time, we often find it was a period of great personal growth, and our lives are much richer for it.

If you are attentive, you can sometimes see the step another person is waiting to take in life. She will start to attract situations that contain the lesson she needs to learn. If the lesson goes unlearned, more traumatic situations are attracted, sometimes in the form of a divorce, illness, or accident.

Events of this magnitude are effective teachers.

But must we learn through pain? The events that lead me to write this book grew out of pain. An area of my life needed attention but I refused to face it. The known pain was more comfortable than the unknown resolution.

Then the messenger came–he knocked and knocked again. I resisted. The Universe had given me explicit lessons in the past on how life works, but still I didn't pay attention–until I awoke panic stricken in the middle of the night. I stood at the edge of an abyss of darkness, clinging to the world I knew by sheer force of will. Finally I surrendered to the Messenger. My stance: "Don't hit me, I'll go peacefully!"

Once I had committed to facing my life, I made myself available to follow whatever path was pointed out. This book is on that path. My present challenge is to stay one step ahead of the Messenger–and to learn from joy instead of pain.

Several years ago, at the Bread 'n Roses Cafe, I met a woman named Sandra who was unhappy in her job as a sales representative. When I suggested she expand her horizons to other possibilities rather than be miserable, she said, "Well, I guess things aren't bad enough yet to motivate me to do something."

Hearing her response, I was happy not to be in her shoes. She could change jobs or change the way she perceives her present work. However, ignoring the messenger who brings internal conflict is done at grave risk.

Anguish is resistance to the flow of life. It is the messenger's knock. Heed it. Look to see what situation is causing your suffering. Then face the problem and ask the messenger to lead the way.

Resolving inner conflict may not have anything to do with changing your situation. It may be as simple as accepting life as it is and moving on, rather than resisting. Or the situation may demand a dramatic change, though you fear its consequences. You don't have to figure out a solution. All you have to do is move in the direction shown and resolution will occur.

Once a fundamental problem has been addressed, motion enters and transformation occurs.

≈ 8 ≈

DESIRE
DEMOTED

Satisfy one desire, another appears.

Desire is natural and familiar. It can be a balanced part of our lives–or a demanding tyrant. A thirsty man's desire for water is appropriate. Desire to drive a Jaguar, wear the latest designer fashions, or acquire expensive furniture is another matter.

Desire is often a distraction we create to avoid dealing with the real issues in our lives. Unfortunately, avoiding problems can cause them to increase in intensity. Continued avoidance is countered by spawning more desires. A vicious circle is created in which desire runs our lives.

Suppose you are unhappy with your job but it provides a comfortable and secure living. You have a well-paid position and are afraid to quit and look for more meaningful work. To lift your spirits, you treat yourself to a great stereo system. This acquisition makes you happy for about week–then the underlying unhappiness returns. To

55

stave it off, you buy a new car. Still the unhappiness returns.

Shopping malls are full of people attempting to shop their way to happiness. Unfortunately, you cannot buy your way out of unhappiness.

As one desire is satisfied, another takes its place. Satisfying desire creates only a brief interlude of contentment. Continued desire creates an inner tension that robs you of the "now" in your life. It becomes the master and you the slave.

At this point you might elect to try the path of "no desire". You do this by carefully examining each desire as it arises and gently putting it aside. After all, you know any satisfaction derived by acquiescing to desire will be transitory.

As desires keep arising and being put aside, you find you have to keep your guard up all the time. Desire becomes the enemy, and material goods are viewed with suspicion— as the weapons of desire. Now you meet your greatest enemy, the desire to be without desire, and you are lost.

Doing without material goods is often an attempt to distract us from the conditions of our lives, just as acquiring them can be. We may have underlying feelings of guilt, inadequacy, or spiritual impurity. In this case, there is an attempt to feel better about oneself by rejecting the rewards of life. Acquiring or rejecting material things in an attempt to feel better is completely beside the point if it has nothing to do with the problem.

The "path of desire" and the "path of no desire" can be

one and the same. They can both be attempts to avoid the issue.

Is it possible to master desire? No, but you can make it your ally. You can desire to be complete and without internal conflict–and pursue this desire relentlessly. To be complete is the act of embracing each moment without the desire for it to be different than it is. To be relentless in the pursuit of completeness is the act of accepting each moment with out resistance, self-pity, or attachment. As this ability matures, inner conflict subsides.

When living life without resistance, life flows. Material goods come and go as needed to enhance the natural expression of existence. Desire is no longer an issue; you are interested only in "living" as you revel in the beauty, mystery, and magic of it all.

UNREASONABLE JOY

To be happy without a reason is unreasonable.

Have you ever been asked, "What are you so happy about?" when you were having an especially good day? That person assumed your joy was based on recent events–and that may have been right.

We are generally happy when things go well and unhappy when things go poorly.

But aren't good and bad subjective? You can make a homeless man happy by taking him to a restaurant for a hot meal. If you take your boss to the same restaurant, he may think, "They overcooked my steak and the service is poor".

Faced with similar events, different people have different reactions. Some choose to be happy while others choose misery. The choice will depend on where they are "coming from", but almost everyone will make a choice.

Todd comes home after work and is greeted by his wife, Molly.

"Honey, you won't believe this." she says, "We won a trip to Hawaii in a supermarket drawing."

He is thrilled.

"By the way," she says, "the repair man came to check the refrigerator today. He said it is not worth fixing, and we should get a new one."

Todd becomes upset

"Oh," she continues, "Billy received the highest mark in his class on a math test."

He feels better—until she adds, "Some old guy that could hardly see backed into the car today while I was shopping."

This is a never-ending story that goes on and on.

Are we victims of fate that must ride this emotional roller coaster to our deaths, or is there another way?

Looking back, what changed for Todd as Molly recited the litany of the day's events? Nothing. She talked and he reacted to what was said.

What practical alternative exists? The way of unreasonable joy. When you follow this path you greet each event as an opportunity for learning. Events are not labeled "good" or "bad", but are viewed as part of the learning process.

I was visiting my friend Madeline at her office when her accountant called to tell her that he had finished her income tax return and she owed the IRS $6000. Without skipping a beat, she said, "I can pay this bill and be angry–or I can just pay it". She chose not to suffer.

When faced with adversity, she often says, "Great! Another opportunity for enlightenment!"

If you follow Madeline's path, it is more difficult to see "bad"–and as "bad" disappears so does "good". Internal turmoil subsides and a deep sense of joy wells up. It is joy-without-reason, joy that is free of the vagaries of fate.

But can we really live this way on a daily basis? Suppose someone close to you dies. Are you really going to feel joy? Feel whatever you feel, cry as much as you like until the pain subsides and then raise your head, look around and ask: "What can I learn?" "What is new in this experience?" Do not waste such a powerful event.

The pain of loss is a direct experience. Thinking about the pain of loss and wallowing in self-pity are the mental habits of a victim and can be dropped. Dropping these habits leaves room for "unreasonable joy" to return.

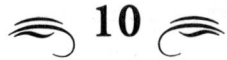

10

EGO UNDONE

Discover who you are, not who think you are.

The lion of the savanna is a beast of beauty, power, and grace. He is not confused about the purpose of life or how to go about living it. No one suggests the "King of the Beasts" has an ego problem. The lion does what comes naturally and fulfills a role that is an important part of the integrated whole. The same is true of the field mouse.

Aboriginal societies of hunters and gatherers, some of which still exist, consider themselves to be an integrated part of the environment and live accordingly. Industrial-man, or more recently technological-man, is more confused about his natural role.

It is evident from the way we live that we often consider ourselves as a separate, non-integrated part of our environment. This view is at least partly responsible for what

we call "ego". When we see someone acting in an aggressive or arrogant way, we may ascribe it to the ego with
observations like, "He's on an ego trip." People who are
driven to succeed are sometimes perceived as having an
"ego problem".

There is an underlying uneasiness that the ego, whatever
it is, is the source of some, if not all, of our problems.

To escape inner turmoil, we may look to the eastern
notion of "no self" or "egolessness". Of course, not
having experienced this, we don't really know what it
means. Our experiments with "egolessness" generally
start by trying to get rid of our ego. Since we perceive
that we are in a state of "separateness", we assume there is
a battle to be fought with our ego, after which we will be
one with everything else. Our notions of "oneness", of
course, have nothing to do with the experience of oneness
and only serve as more grist for the mill of thinking mind.
Thus we become a battleground and are further from our
goal of inner peace than ever.

To do battle with our ego, we first attempt to expose the
enemy. This is not easy since we aren't sure what it is.
While it is easy to observe the ego at work in our fellows,
it is difficult to pin it down in ourselves. We lie in wait,
watching for ego to show itself. We notice that when we
accomplish something grand there is a sense of pride that
"I" did this, and the ego is revealed. The more unique the
accomplishment, the more the ego is exposed.

Now we have identified the enemy: it is the sense of
unique accomplishment, for without this, pride (or
blame) would not arise, and the perception of "I" doing
something would not be present. Without a "me" observ-

ing myself, I would be the natural animal I was meant to be and experience unity and peace.

At this point we are in a lot of trouble. The only way to kill the ego is to kill ourselves. In the immortal words of Pogo, "we have met the enemy, and he is us!" Let us hope we can find a way out.

Uniqueness is not illusion; it is a non-negotiable fact. Just as every snowflake is unique, so is every physical form. Just as snowflakes make up snow, individual uniqueness makes up the human experience. This is the beauty of creation.

Your greatest gift to the Universe is to be uniquely you! A total embracing of uniqueness shows deep appreciation for the gift of life. Those old Zen masters were unique, and their uniqueness shines down through the centuries to light our way. "Oneness" is not the absence of unique- ness, but recognition of the connectedness of all things.

Thinking Mind, however, is still faced with the paradox of "oneness" and "separation". After all, we know living in "separation" is painful, and we hope desperately that there is such a thing as "unity" which will bring us peace.

Conflicts are seldom resolved by fighting battles. If we view each battle separately, we have the illusion of win- ning or losing. However, viewed as a continuum, as one battle ends the seed for the next is planted, and we have a long, never ending battle.

How does this relate to the path of "no self?" Any plan for realizing success must proceed along the lines of no resistance. Ego is an illusion that does not have to be defeated; it only has to be dropped. The key to the dilemma is that the path of "no self" is the path of no self-image and has nothing to do with uniqueness. The real culprit is self-image created by thinking mind.

The problem is not that I am unique or that I find joy in this. The problem is—I think I know who I am. Who I am is not a thinking matter—it is an experience. If I live in the self-image I create, then infinite possibilities are reduced to a handful of finite possibilities. I lose the fluidity and grace of the lion and become the paralyzed prey of my own mind.

Creation is a never-ending dance of energies. In order to dance, we must be free to move without restriction. In this dance, my self-image is like wearing clothes that are way too tight. No matter how attractive, it limits the kind of dancing I can do.

We spend much of our lives trying to be "somebody". If you go to a celebrity party, you will see a lot of people "being" celebrities. At an office party, you will find managers "being" managers and underlings being eager, rising professionals.

At a cocktail party people ask, "What do you do?" which is their way of asking, "Who are you?"

Many professionals do what they do so they will have an acceptable identity. This is their way of creating a comfortable self-image. Without it, they feel adrift and insecure. With it, they are like the Wizard of Oz, little people hiding behind the control panels of their public identities.

Some people say, "I know myself." Forget it! The only

way to know who you are is to forget who you think you are. The way to freedom is to drop self-image. As you drop self-image, you drop self-imposed boundaries. As you drop boundaries, you drop judgments. As you drop judgments, the mind has less grist for its mill and must become quiet.

Now you can experience the moment, and experience the uniqueness. Now you can experience you and guess what?

"You" disappear.

≈ 11 ⇒

L O V E

The critical issue with love is that we must start with ourselves–loving others without loving yourself is like building a house without a foundation. Loving yourself is much more difficult than loving someone else. After all, you know too many of your own secrets and foibles. You may want to be better looking, more honest, more loving, more intelligent, and a gourmet cook–everything that you find attractive.

But if you can love yourself exactly as you are at this instant, then you can love the perfection of the Universe. Each of us in our uniqueness allows for an experience that could not exist otherwise and, as such, is a great gift to the human consciousness.

After all, you are the human experience. As you accept yourself, you open up channels for greater awareness and the opportunity for a new experience of spiritual prosperity. This has nothing to do with being holy; it has only to do with embracing life. Similarly, it may have nothing to do with money, for when you prosper in the spirit you follow the path that is revealed knowing your needs will be met.

Loving yourself is one key to personal transformation. This self-love encompasses more than you might think.

First, you must act in ways that allow you to truly like yourself. This is not a matter of doing what you think is "right" out of a sense of obligation. It is, instead, acting out of a sense of your deepest truth, since this is what really brings you joy. This can be very difficult, since your innermost truths often require you to take a risk and act in other than conventional patterns.

A second aspect of loving yourself is to distinguish between those acts that make you "feel good" and those that make you feel good about yourself. If something makes you "feel good" but leaves you with guilt, then, for the moment at least, you are not acting in a way that allows you to love yourself most fully. In this sense, self-love is based on self-discipline.

Self-love may be defined as the absence of inner conflict. This brings us to a third aspect of self-love, which is forgiveness and acceptance. It is important that you not berate yourself for who you are or have been, but accept the miracle of yourself and continually move in the direction of fulfillment.

You may be afraid to love yourself because you are not all you want to be and are afraid if you accept yourself you will never be any different. In fact, it is much more difficult to make real changes if you are wasting your energy condemning some part of yourself. You can be much stronger if you accept yourself, appreciate the lessons learned by being exactly who you are, and choose what new experience you wish to have by moving in that direction.

Loving yourself has nothing to do with being conceited or arrogant. In arrogance, you put yourself above others, and generally find that there are others, who have more of what you want to put above yourself. Some people are so arrogant that no one is good enough for them, including themselves! This is the ultimate extreme and is a great gift, for there is no where to go from here but death or resolution! Resolution, if it comes, is the experience of total unity.

Loving ourselves is the foundation for loving others. This doesn't mean you will no longer observe dishonesty, arrogance, or whatever else presently offends you in other people. It just means that when you see these traits, no negative reaction arises. Instead, you observe these as elements of personality some have chosen on their path to greater awareness.

As your personal clarity increases, you may even see the lessons this person is learning through these traits. This provides the opportunity to learn by observation rather than suffering the pain of the experience yourself. You can then be grateful for the insight provided by these people being exactly who they are. In that moment you can thank them and love them for being themselves. At this point you no longer love others for whom they are, or are not, but love them because they are.

Loving someone does not obligate you to be partners with

them, spend time with them, or give them what they ask for. Love is not attached to obligation; it is an energy that flows through us.

Now let's talk about what most of us are really interested in, Romantic Love. Many of us use this kind of love like a drug. If life is lonely and empty, we look for someone to fall in love with. If we are successful, fine–for a while. At some point, we must come to terms with the fact that the person we are in love with is not who we thought. After all, the person we fell in love with does not exist! We made this person up to fit the role required to fill the empty space in our life, and then assumed the person before us was the object of our affection. As the real person surfaces through the image we have created, we may or may not choose to continue to be in love with him or her. More often than not, we feel greatly disappointed, distressed, and betrayed. We then fall out of love.

The crucial point here is that romantic love is not something that happens to us, it is a choice we make! We may choose to do this for any number of reasons, but they are not the reasons we usually admit to. The difficulty with this arrangement is that we may have a hidden agenda of needs that our partner is supposed to satisfy. This is often unsuccessful because of who our partner is, as opposed to who we want our partner to be, as well as the fact that we have not admitted to our own agenda.

A woman I know was undecided about moving in with her boyfriend and making the relationship more permanent. She said that while she liked and enjoyed him, he wasn't exactly her idea of Prince Charming. When I asked her to describe Prince Charming, she said, "My Prince Charming has good looks, a successful career, is affluent, tender, sensitive, and has a zest for life". It occurred to me that she had listed all the things she herself wanted to be but didn't feel she was.

If we all work toward accepting ourselves and being our own Prince or Princess charming, then we may satisfy our own needs. We could then be available to love a companion for being the person they truly are, and this would be romantic indeed.

Am I suggesting that romantic love is not possible over a long period of time? Not at all. I know a number of people who have very long-standing romantic relationships. However, you are not much good to someone else until you are good to yourself. When you are in harmony, you can be a strong partner. When you can be a strong partner, then you can have a strong partner. This is the foundation for a romantic love that will stand the test of time.

≈ 12 ⊱

F E A R

Fear of death is, for many people, the ultimate fear.
Often, the attraction of religion is that it describes life
after death, thus making it less of an unknown, and so,
less fearful. Death, however, is at least certain and is
sometimes less frightening than the uncertainty of life.
There is a constant effort on our part to keep ourselves in
familiar surroundings, even though those surroundings
may be painful. Our lives are often a valiant attempt to
keep ourselves safe for death, which we hope will come
upon us unaware in our sleep.

But, to experience joy, love, and unity in our lives, we
must be willing to move into the unknown–the thing we
fear the most! The life force itself is a river of energy
which cannot be known, it can only be experienced. True
joy comes when we are willing to flow freely with this
energy and become one with the marvel and mystery of it.

Thinking about it, when you are fearful, it is always based on fear for the future. You may dread something you have experienced in the past, but the thing you fear is recurrence in the future. We are afraid of the unknown of the future but must face it or die. What a dilemma—is there anything we can do?

Fear's vulnerability is that it only has meaning in terms of what hasn't yet happened and may never happen. Since fear relates to the future, which is unknown, its only ally is Thinking Mind acting as a bridge between what exists, and what you fear. As the mind is quieted, and appropriate action is revealed, fear—even if it is present—does not paralyze you.

When you act from a sense of "inner knowing", you act with trust and confidence. Your confidence is not that you won't suffer pain or death, but that you are acting in harmony with the forces of the Universe.

When operating in this manner fear becomes your ally. It alerts you to possible danger, it heightens your sense of the moment, but fear does not defeat you. Nor do you defeat it—instead you move with it.

If you are about to cross the street and see a car coming, do you put fear aside and cross anyway? Only if you are anxious to get yourself killed.

You shouldn't ignore fear any more than you should ignore the pain from putting your hand on a hot stove. It is a signal something is going on that you should know about.

Accepting the presence of fear does not mean you must lead a fearful life. Fear is an emotion, and its presence is not a problem—it can be an ally and a teacher. It is only when you move out of the realm of appropriate action and become paralyzed by fear that you have a problem. In this case, fear becomes the master and can cause you to cower in the dark recesses of your imagination rather than flourishing in the sunlight.

My friend, Ann, is very successful in her career as a corporate manager. She feels her position is especially significant, since she is succeeding in what has historically been a man's world. Unfortunately, her work is not satisfying. Life lacks meaning, and she is not contributing to the solution of problems she sees in the world around her. Ann told me that she is afraid to leave her position and look for meaningful work.

If fear is the master, she will go to her grave feeling the slave. On the other hand, if she acts from the wisdom of silent mind, life will be brand new and sparkling every moment, even though she may be scared silly.

I was once in a similar situation. I visited my mother shortly after she had open-heart surgery (in 1968 when such procedures were still making headlines). She had changed drastically from the woman I knew as my mother. She was serene and kind beyond words, without any fuss. She radiated peace, with nothing pending and nothing to hang on to. Death could come at any moment and, in the meantime, she had life, which she savored in a quiet way.

We were having lunch in her kitchen when she said, "Francis, you disappoint me".

I couldn't believe what I was hearing, especially since I appeared successful and was the most "normal" of all my brothers and sisters. She continued, "You don't like your job, but you won't quit because you're afraid you'll starve. You're selling your life for a couple of measly bucks!"

Needless to say, she got my attention, and life has been more interesting ever since.

Fear is an emotion that sustains our view of separateness. Unity is the unknown and so can be a very uncomfortable concept. After all, if life and death are not separate, then don't we have to accept death? If sickness and health are not separate, mustn't we accept sickness? If there is no separateness, how can we push away all those things we have judged to be bad?

The question we would like to leave unasked is, can we push these things away anyway? Do you see anyone successfully pushing away sickness, death, or any of the other situations we find so traumatic in our lives?

Resisting life's situations is much like Brer Rabbit punching the Tar Baby—the more you fight it, the more you are stuck to it.

If we assume completeness is to be found in the moment as it exists, without change, then we have to view sickness as just sickness, pain as just pain, death as just death, and fear as just fear. In this case, you are not pain, you are not death, and you are not fear, you are just you.

There is no denying we live in a world saturated with fear. Our international policy is based on it. We have thousands of nuclear weapons on twenty-four hour standby to be launched at a moment's notice. Likewise, we have thousands of these warheads aimed at us. We live in the shadow of complete annihilation. We fear that we are polluting our environment and using up our resources. We fear the effects of our national deficit and our trade deficit. We fear crime in the streets, cancer, and AIDS. There seems to be no shortage of things to be afraid of—there is something for everyone. Many powerful politicians, corporate presidents, and military generals may be driven by fear of failure–the fear of not being enough.

The fear of our times is communicated to all parts of the globe through the modern miracle of television. Now is our opportunity to see fear as a teacher, for we have in our midst the very powerful teacher–worldwide fear. If fear is the teacher, what is the teaching? There is only one thing that can conquer fear, and that is love.

We must learn and embrace the teaching before the opportunity is past.

≈ 13 ≈

GUILT
AS GURU

If every emotion can be a teacher as well as an experience, let's see what guilt has to teach us.

Guilt arises when we do something we think is wrong or don't do something we believe is right. Many people believe that guilt is a necessary instrument of conscience which helps to keep us from wreaking (even more) havoc upon our fellow man. After all, if it weren't for guilt, a cornerstone of some prominent modern religions, there might be a tremendous upsurge of raping, pillaging and general disruption. But, does guilt hold us back from committing crimes, eating too much, or cheating on taxes? Guilt has seldom deterred me. In the past, I gave in to temptation easily and then tortured myself with guilt and remorse. I became quick to find fault and ready to blame those closest to me. Guilt did not make me loving or lovable.

Likewise, guilt has not made the world free of violence and is not likely to do so. The tormented mind seldom spawns loving action.

Am I suggesting guilt is bad? Not at all–guilt is a teacher. The question is how do we learn from it? First recognize that the anguish of guilt is a messenger and should be given our attention. It tells us there is resistance to something in ourselves or the world that is ready to be faced. When we feel guilt, we know the teacher has arrived, and it is a time to be silent and learn.

Recognize that guilt does not arise because you have done something wrong, but because you have done something you believe is wrong. For instance, two overweight people eat ice cream cones; one feels guilty, and one does not. Both people engaged in the same act, but they have different belief systems relative to that act.

When guilt comes, it is telling you something about your belief system. You can use this to point out those things that you do not accept about the world and about yourself. A deeper acceptance can come if one is willing to go within and listen for understanding.

This does not mean you should continue to act badly in the face of guilt! Quite the contrary, you should stop and face the issue guilt is pointing out. Maybe you no longer wish to be overweight and are ready to give up ice cream! The point is that it is not wrong to eat ice cream, it just may not be appropriate for you. Guilt may be a signal that what you are doing is no longer useful to you.

There is so much resistance to facing some issues in our lives that we may purposely engage in activities we can feel guilty about as a diversionary tactic. My friend, Alex, had a very unsatisfactory relationship with his wife. As the problems became more obvious, he began to gamble compulsively—often for days at a time. He felt tremendous guilt over his obsessive gambling but would not stop. The gambling compounded his problems with the marriage, and his life became a living Hell.

For Alex, gambling was a secondary issue on which he could attach the guilt he felt over the failing marriage. However, diverting attention from the fundamental problem was a weak tactic that, because of his heavy losses, nearly ended in disaster. When he was finally forced to face the issues concerning the marriage, he began to regain balance in his life. Gambling reverted to being just gambling, and while he continues to gamble occasionally, it no longer controls his life.

Many of us are not willing to change our behavior patterns because they represent the known and comfortable world. Guilt may be something we hang onto because we are not ready to change and learn the lesson presented. To use guilt as an effective teacher, one must be willing to face the issue defined by guilt and resolve it.

Let go of the notion of doing things because they are "right" and not doing things because they are "wrong". Rather suspend the judgments of thinking and begin to act from a sense of appropriate action.

When you do what is appropriate, your actions feel harmonious and powerful. As these feelings arise, guilt dissipates and its work is done.

SPIRITUALITY

Do you think of yourself as a spiritual person? I hope so, for indeed you are. But how about the thief, the wino, the murderer?

Two young Zen monks were crossing the monastery grounds when they were horrified to see an old monk urinating on the statue of the Buddha. "Stop! Stop! You're peeing on the Buddha!" they cried, hoping to halt this outrageous act of senility. Alarmed, the old monk grabbed himself and stopped the flow. "Quick," he yelled back, "I have to go real bad! Show me where the Buddha isn't."

If one is of the spirit, aren't we all? Can we pick and choose?

Nothing exists that is not of the spirit and in its rightful place. Many of our saints were reformed sinners; the potential is always there. Everyone is participating in his or her own way, and we appear to be moving toward a common meeting place of a fuller awareness.

If all things are of the spirit, does this mean that it is okay to lead a life of dissipation? If satisfying your lust sounds like more fun than praying, then satisfy your lust! After all, why pray and meditate? Is it to do someone a favor or to appear holy? No good can come of anything until you are able to do it with a full and open heart.

St. Francis of Assisi is reputed to have led a life of considerable debauchery until he finally concluded there was no hope of finding true fulfillment in this manner. He was then moved to seek God and came to the realization that God is in all things. Debauchery had served its purpose and was no longer useful to him.

There is another story about a Zen master who, upon seeing a monk meditating in the garden called out, "Why are you sitting there?"

"To become the Buddha", came the reply.

"You can no more become the Buddha by sitting there than you can empty the ocean with a teacup," responded the master.

Sitting silently is no more spiritual than sitting on a barstool. Sitting silently is merely a technique for quieting Thinking Mind. We don't have to perform spiritual acts to be spiritual; we already are spiritual! We need only to discover our spirituality and that of everything around us to live in unreasonable joy.

This does not mean meditation is without value. Many

have come to discover the spirit-in-all-things through meditation. The point is this: if you make meditation a moral issue, you create separation between those who meditate and those who don't, and separation is limitation.

Spirituality is not about morality or merit. Spirituality is recognizing the spirit in all things and experiencing unity rather than separation. Then you are free to wander without judging and be a source of light to all who need it. Enlightenment is nothing more than this.

∾ 15 ∾

RESPONSIBILITY

We often view our lives as a struggle in which our dreams and desires are either achieved or pulled from our grasp by fate. When things go well, we congratulate ourselves and take public bows. When things go poorly, we curse those forces that have power over us and fall into the depths of despair. In this scheme of things, we are victims—orphan children who can never relax. No matter how successful we are, we must continue to pit ourselves against the forces of the universe.

If I say to you, "You must take responsibility for your life," the word responsibility will have a particular meaning. Responsibility may conjure up thoughts of a nose-to-the-grindstone work ethic, well-planned insurance coverage, money saved for the kids` college education or savings for retirement. In this case, responsibility is a tricky thing for how do you know when you have sacrificed enough and saved enough? Since you can never be sure, you are caught in a web of uncertainty.

You have taken upon yourself the responsibility to make the world safe for yourself and those dependent on you, with no escape clause. Unfortunately, the world is not safe—you are fighting a losing battle.

How different life becomes if each situation is viewed as an opportunity to experience completeness. If you accept the challenge of the moment and assume that appropriate action will arise, responsibility is very simple and unambiguous. You take responsibility by considering each situation as a gift and an opportunity for greater learning and by accepting the consequences of your actions (or inaction) without regret or self-pity. Thus you never give up your power to outside sources by considering yourself a victim, and your resolve is never weakened by self-pity.

This notion of responsibility is supported by the assumption that there is such a thing as "right action". That is, there is an appropriate response to every situation and further, you can know what this right action is through an inner awareness. If you perform what you believe to be the "right action" in each circumstance, you have no reason for regret.

As we examine this approach to responsibility, many questions arise. For instance, since this approach has no "moral" guidelines, isn't it possible one would perform some terrible act he would later regret? On the contrary, "terrible" acts are more likely to be committed by those who are not seeking Clear Mind and completeness than those who are.

This is true because most of the acts that we consider terrible are committed based on thoughts of persecution, greed, revenge, or moral righteousness. These thoughts are Thinking Mind's attempt to sustain its view of separateness in the world. As we pursue our own totality, this view of the world collapses and such thoughts begin to lose their power over us. In their place arise feelings of joy, mystery, wonder, and completeness.

One might pose the question: "If the 'seeker' is so attuned to the moment, does this mean she wouldn't carry insurance, have a savings account, a pension fund, or an IRA fund?" Not at all—it just means she does not consider planning as taking responsibility for her life. Planning is just planning. If she feels planning or saving is appropriate, then she will do that. The difference between her actions and those of most people is that she acts out of a sense of "appropriateness" without any expectations. Therefore, if after fifty years of contributing to the pension fund the company folds and all benefits are lost, she is not crushed by bitterness, despair, and self-pity but proceeds, as she has always proceeded, with awe, wonder, and trust.

≈ 16 ≈

TRUE
SERVICE

An act of service is action that springs from a loving heart.

As you move through life, a desire to do something
meaningful often arises, the desire to make a difference by
helping those around you. Some people spend their lives
as social workers or volunteer for worthwhile projects in
the community. We would like to think these efforts
derive from true selflessness, but the motivation is often
something quite different.

Service may be rendered out of a feeling of obligation, a
need to appear righteous, a desire to be needed, or any
number of other reasons. The question is, what is truly of
service and does anything really help?

In order to be of service, you must be able to clearly
perceive the needs of others. This is not easy, since in
most cases we perceive how our own needs can be met
through "helping" others rather than perceiving their
needs. So we serve others in an attempt to fill our own
needs through the activity of service–often with little

success– and everyone remains needy.

Does this mean nothing "helps"? Not at all, it only means that true help is the complement of real need.

I recently had a conversation with Ernie, a carnival worker, who received room and board during the winter months in return for preparing and serving meals to the homeless. Ernie was very proud of the fact that the street people, mostly alcoholics, much preferred the food and atmosphere he was helping to provide over that of the Salvation Army. Having been "down and out" himself, he served with compassion and without judgment or moralizing. Both parties took part in an act of compassion and no one felt deficient.

In order to be of true service, drop pity for others just as you dropped self-pity. Said in a different way, feeling sorry for someone doesn't help him or her any more than self-pity can help you.

This does not mean one can not be of service; it just means that pity is without real power. Compassionate action that springs from a loving heart is of much greater service than good intentions born of pity. The challenge is to render service from completeness rather than inner need.

We often think of the human circumstance as tragic because so many people are in a state of need and death is never far away. In the larger view, "need" acts as a vacuum that draws in those with something to give. As the two unite, a synergistic bond is formed which makes the "whole" greater than the sum of its parts.

Those who have felt the joy of service almost always say that they receive more than they can possibly give.

Lisa, a friend who does volunteer work with the terminally ill, confided that she does it because she is selfish. She says no matter how much she gives, she receives more in return. Her life overflows with the joy derived from this work and she can no longer imagine life without it.

True service is the loving action that unites the donor and the recipient.

We usually associate being of service with situations where the need is obvious. Situations where people are starving, homeless, sick or dying, to name a few. However, there is often an opportunity to be of service in more subtle circumstances. In fact, to be of service in many little ways in our everyday life is probably a more powerful force for transformation than any single act of self-sacrifice.

The saying "charity begins at home" is especially appropriate since it is sometimes the most difficult to be charitable with those who are closest to you.

An accountant once said to me, "I have learned more about dysfunctional families from preparing income tax returns than is found in most books on the subject. Many married couples come to me to have their tax statements prepared. It is amazing to watch the drama of the marital relationship unfold before my eyes. The couples are seldom truly kind to each other. One person is almost always dominant and asserts that dominance time and again. Both parties engage in undermining the other's confidence and trust." This is not a particularly up-lifting view of relationships, but it is probably accurate.

The "glue" that holds many marriages together is the feeling of security it provides and, as a result, many of us do whatever we can to make our partner more insecure and so, more dependent. This results in the "can't live with them and can't live without them" syndrome of which we are so fond.

If marriage partners made every effort to be of loving service to their spouses, the opportunities for transformation would be limitless.

We often have the opportunity to be of service when we are being served. How many times have you been confronted by an unhappy servant of the public at the license bureau, post office, or in a restaurant? Instead of being angry at the rude service, you can smile or say a sympathetic word.

This doesn't mean you feel sorry for the person, or even that your compassionate approach will be appreciated. It only means that you have given a gift in the name of service.

My friend, Steve, miraculously escaped serious injury when he drove off the road to avoid a head-on collision. The other car also went off the road and sustained some damage although no one was injured. The car was driven by a local young "tough" who, along with his two friends, was drunk.

Steve was furious, mostly at the thought of what would happen to his wife and children if he were killed. He is extremely muscular (a blacksmith by trade) and was anxious to teach the drunken driver a lesson. However, the police came before he could commit mayhem on the young men. He decided to bide his time since he lives in a small town and knew he would see these fellows again.

About a week later, Steve walked into a local tavern and there were the same three getting drunk again. They recognized the blacksmith and expected the worst. He motioned for them to step outside and they sullenly complied.

However, my friend had a problem. He wasn't afraid of the three-to-one odds because it was obvious he was in the right, and these young men were already defeated psychologically. But he had recently become a born-again Christian, and here he was about to beat up on his fellow man. What a dilemma! As he was walking outside he kept asking himself, "What would Christ do in this situation?"

The tavern opened onto a courtyard where the young men stood together like the black sheep that they were. The blacksmith looked at them in a righteous manner and said, "You guys almost killed me the other day and here you are getting drunk again. I'll let you go if you get out of here right now, but I want you to go to church with me on Sunday!" No one, including my friend who had said it, expected this, and they all stood around dumbfounded. Finally, the leader of the young men spoke up and said they would show up at the church at the appropriate time.

Steve phoned the pastor to tell him what he had done. "That's just fine. Don't worry about a thing," the pastor told him. On Sunday the three young men showed up looking scrubbed and very much ill at ease in their Sunday clothes. Once inside the church, the pastor asked everyone to gather around the newcomers to pray and welcome them. As everyone joined in prayer, the young men began to cry. They were not used to being loved.

My understanding is they have become members of the church and continue to attend. Steve had indeed found the essence of the loving heart of Christ and was able to be of service in an unusual manner.

Another place where the opportunity for rendering service is often overlooked is in our work. Many times as we become successful in our careers our focus is on continuing to prove how exceptional we are by attempting to get more and more work out of our subordinates. Our emphasis is often on power, status, and salary rather than personal fulfillment. Let me propose a different scenario.

Let's suppose that you are an executive of a large manufacturing company. During your drive to work, you think about the day's agenda. You set the priorities for your various duties in order to maximize your effectiveness. You are very aware of how your contribution and that of your subordinates relates to the bottom line profit. You know many of the employees look upon executives such as yourself as "fat cats" that are only interested in profit, but you also know that without profit the company will go bankrupt, and the workers will be without jobs.

You are not untypical of the thousands of executives going to work this morning. Many of them are further gearing up to participate in the "dog eat dog" world of industry in order to "bring home the bacon". This requires a gradual transformation from the husband and father who leaves home to the "Vice President in Charge of Manufacturing" who arrives at work. In this regard, you are different. You are the same person at work as at home.

As you enter the building where you work, you notice that most of the other VPs have already arrived and are standing around in small groups chatting. A few of the younger managers are also present. The president of the company arrives shortly after you, and this is the signal for everyone to join hands in a large circle. The president now leads the group, which says in unison: "I choose to be of service to those around me in all of my thoughts, words, and deeds. I maintain a clear mind, sound body, and loving heart in order to accomplish this. I am deeply grateful for the rewards granted me for doing that which brings me overwhelming joy."

This company is different. You still have to pay attention to detail, deliver a quality product on time, and make a profit, but it is no longer work. You are being rewarded for performing a service that you enjoy providing. Do I know of such a company? No, I invented this scenario, but I do know of some that are close, and I wouldn't be surprised if such a place exists. Some of my executive friends certainly embody the principles illustrated. Let's face it, being of service is fun. If you bring service into the work place, everything you do is easier. My experience has been that everyone is more focused and productive and profits are easier to come by. Executive positions become less about being the boss and more about using your talent and experience to lead those under you to success. The financial and professional success you achieve becomes a reward for service rendered rather than a status symbol. You are able to enjoy this reward fully because it results from a labor of love.

Is this vision naive and unrealistic? Well, I know of some powerful executives that operate with a similar vision, and they have been successful. I know others that have achieved success by taking a "hard line". The difference is they work harder and enjoy it less.

We all know the old adage "It is better to give than to receive". I think this is better stated in the prayer of St. Francis, quoted by E. Eswaren in Meditation, as, "It is through giving that we receive."

It is not better to give than receive; they are both part of the whole. When you give, you also receive. My friend Bruce, when offered something generally replies, "Never stifle a generous impulse! I accept."

Receiving graciously is also an act of service.

An act of service has the power to transform both the donor and the recipient. In order to be of service, we must be able to perceive the needs of others clearly. This is most easily done if we are complete in ourselves. When we have dropped our own desperation, we become available to others. As we are available with Clear Mind, we are surprised to find that many people are asking for something other than what they need. They may be asking for money when they need love. They may be asking for love when they need self-esteem, and on and on.

The challenge, in this case, is to use our clarity to help the person find and fill his or her real need. This attempt is not always greeted enthusiastically. People often create problems for a reason and are not necessarily ready to resolve them.

Be that as it may, if one acts from clear mind and with a loving heart, these efforts will be of service.

⤳ 17 ⤵

D E A T H

The Universe, in its wisdom, has provided life with death—as an inexorable fact.

One way of looking at death is that it is the solution to all of life's problems. Some people choose this ultimate solution through suicide, but this is not of interest to the person seeking life—knowing death will have its way all too soon.

What are my credentials for discussing death—what do I know about it? Nothing, of course!
I've been with dying people, and they have told me things. I've talked with people who have been revived after being clinically dead and they have told me things, but I've never had a dead person tell me anything. I guess we would have to agree that all of my information is, at best, third hand. Nonetheless, I'll push on.

I recently had a discussion with a friend on the subject of death. She said that we live many lives on this earth until we learn the lessons that lead to total enlightenment. We are then able to transcend death and ascend to other planes of existence with our physical bodies. There are a number of historical accounts suggesting that this may be the case. The most famous example in our tradition is, of course, the resurrection of Christ. I was quite surprised to find out that there are many other similar claims. A disciple of the Tibetan master Milarepa, who lived about a thousand years ago, left a written account of his Master's life, death, and ascension. Carlos Castaneda refers to his teacher, Don Juan, transcending with his physical body to another plane. Ramtha, the entity channeled by J. Z. Knight, claims to have transcended directly to other realms and states that thousands of others have done the same.

Do I disbelieve these claims? Absolutely not! Do I believe them? Of course not.

A Zen student asked a Korean Zen master, "What is death?" He replied, "You are already dead!" What did he mean? Who knows?

A master swordsman, who was also revered as a man of great understanding, was teaching swordsmanship to a Japanese boy of the Samurai class. One day, the boy asked, "Master, what happens when we die?"
The Master immediately raised his sword above his head and, with a loud war cry, brought it down in a lightning-swift stroke that stopped a hair's breadth from the boy's neck. The boy, expecting to die, let out a blood-curdling scream. The Master smiled and asked, "Do you still want to know?"

One may enlist the power of his death as an ally in discovering the sweet essence of life. For example, if we are immobilized by fear and afraid to take the action that is pointed out by our inner knowing, we can always ask ourselves the question, "what is the worst thing that can happen if I do this?" The answer is, of course, "I can die." But we are going to die anyway, that is a certainty. Since dying is a foregone conclusion, there is not much reason to use it as an excuse for not living.

Casteneda's Don Juan says that the warrior assumes the worst has already happened; he has already died. This gives one tremendous power to concentrate on appropriate action in the moment.

This approach to death has nothing to do with recklessness. The warrior is not interested in cheap thrills–he is interested only in discovering completeness in the moment and pursuing it relentlessly.

I went to visit my father when he was dying of cancer. He said, "I hope this does not bother you; it doesn't bother me. All my life was like climbing a mountain. And then I reached the top. I raised my family and had a full life. Now I am coming down the mountain to die. This is Nature's way, and it is good."

part 2

PREPARING
FOR POWER

I live for this moment,

Every moment;

This is the ridge trail

Which falls off steeply.

One slip means a plunge

Into the abyss of the past

or the future;

Death on both sides,

Step carefully.

Leading a strong life requires self-discipline, a term I used to abhor. My natural (or acquired) distaste for following orders showed itself at an early age. At school I chafed under the imposed discipline and devised a campaign of not-so-subtle resistance–little things like dropping BB's in the aisle during algebra class, water balloons down the stairwell at class-change, taking all the screws out of the desk so it would fall apart when the next person used it, and some others I don't want my kids to know about.

This disruptive behavior caused some of my teachers considerable grief (I hope they are accorded the treatment of saints in the next life, because they deserve it) and, of course, resulted in "disciplinary" action which would further escalate the feud.

Along the way, I confused the ideas of being disciplined and self-discipline. In my fight against one, I began also to resist the other–I threw the baby out with the bath water.

It was easy to fall into undisciplined ways and believe that I was living a "free" life. However, at some point I began to see the truth–my life was disorganized and chaotic. I was accessible to anyone wanting access, even though it was often disruptive, and I lived in the image of what other people wanted me to be. Instead of enjoying my indulgent ways, I felt trapped and resentful.

It took me years to break old habits that fostered weakness and find new ones that nurtured strength. Each step along the way has resulted in a sense of accomplishment and increased well being, which motivates me to continue to work toward a healthier life. This continuing search has turned into a process of discovery, rather than struggle, and provides an exciting challenge as I get older. Leading a stronger life lessens suffering and allows me an opportunity to enjoy the fruits of my labor.

The premise of this book is that a strong life is seldom an accident and is based on a disciplined approach to living. If we make a distinction between the "art" and the "craft" of living, this part of the book is about the craft. It is about leading a life that encourages good health, fitness, and mental acuity, with the assumption that this is the best foundation for creative living.

While it is true that an excellent craftsman may never create great art, it is also true that great art is usually built on a foundation of good craftsmanship–Leonardo Da Vince learned to draw before he created the Mona Lisa, and Nureyev took dance lessons.

When my brother was teaching photography, he told his students, "I can teach you the craft of photography, but the 'art' is up to you". Unfortunately, it would be grandiose for me to claim that I can teach you the craft of living when I am still struggling like everyone else. I have made progress though and will pass on some of the approaches that work for me. We can talk more about the art of living later.

⤜ 18 ⤛

LETTING GO
OF CHAOS

One night, when I was sleeping in a mountain camp-ground, I was awakened by a loud commotion. A truck-load of late arrivals was driving around looking for an empty campsite. The driving was erratic and the shouting of suggestions and directions amongst the party echoed through the campground.

The driver stopped the truck, with lights blazing and motor running, to discuss the situation. Opinions about how to find the right campsite were expressed in loud voices.

All of a sudden, during a brief lull in the noise, a woman's voice pierced the night as she shouted, "Hey people, let's get it together. This is too much fucking chaos!"

I believe her comment is apropos to our lives in general. We are caught up in, and obsessed by, chaos.

There has always been some measure of chaos in the

world. In the past there were sounds of horses trotting, a peddler hawking his wares, or maybe the sound of a blacksmith at work. These were the sounds of the Universe unfolding in a quieter age. The amount of noise and distraction has, however, increased dramatically since the advent of machines and, more recently, modern technology. The world was a much quieter place before cars, airplanes, radios, television, and factories.

In the past, the absence of the chaos of the modern world allowed people to be in much closer contact with their intuitive powers. This is still true in some remote areas as evidenced by, for example, Lorens Van der Post's accounts of the intuitive abilities of the Bushmen of the Kalahari Desert. In some societies spiritual seekers still go off to meditate in the silence of mountain caves, sometimes for years.

In recent times we have become dependent on continual stimulation to stave off feelings of internal disquiet. Many people leave the television on even when it is not being watched because it "keeps them company." We have radios and telephones in our cars. MUZAK follows us wherever we go in stores, restaurants, and even elevators. When you are put on "hold" by a receptionist, you may find yourself listening to a low fidelity rendition of "Greensleeves". We refer to most of this input as "background music". It is not music to listen to; it just keeps the silence at bay. We are not comfortable when things are too quiet.

While hiking in a national forest, I met a fellow wearing headphones. He politely removed them to exchange greetings. My curiosity overcame my sense of propriety, and I asked him what he was listening to on his

Walkman tape player. He replied, "sounds of nature".

The noise around us will not thwart silent mind if we are either detached from it or listening intently to it. However, to continually introduce noise into our environment in order to drive out silence is an act of desperation.

Silence is, to some, boring and at a deeper level, frightening. In silence, they feel alone and abandoned. But true joy can only be found in the moment, and it may reside in the silence.

Revel in the joy of silence. When presented with sound, embrace it or let it roll off you like water, whichever suits your purpose at the moment. Erica's dream (see page 27) tells us, "If you are afraid of sound - listen!" Likewise, if you are afraid of silence - be silent!

Noise is not the only thing we use to distract ourselves. As youngsters we are taught in school that keeping abreast of the daily news is part of our obligation as responsible members of a democratic society. We may even believe it is our patriotic duty to read the newspaper. Over the years many of us develop a newspaper "addiction" and must begin each day with it.

The newspaper is both portable and quiet, so it provides a convenient entertainment in situations where other media are not so acceptable, such as on public transportation or even in the work place. This means we can carry our entertainment with us, even when we are commuting to work.

Let's take a look at the role the newspaper really plays in our lives. Pick up a newspaper, and pretend you have never seen one before. Examine each of the articles intently. How much of the information is of vital importance to your life and how much of it is extraneous? Are you able to read just those items that are vital to you (assuming you have found some), or do other items catch your eye? What effect does the information you read have on you? Do you feel centered, balanced, and in charge when you finish?

My own experience is that most of the information contained in the newspaper has very little to do with my personal life. I can live very nicely without reading a daily newspaper for months on end (I don't follow the stock market very closely). In fact, our society is so saturated with media news it is very difficult not to know what is going on. However, if I do read the newspaper, I find all manner of interesting things to hold my attention. What is wrong with that?

For many of us there is no problem. We are looking for distraction and entertainment. It is our narcotic for avoiding the silence. Unfortunately, the temporary escape from the problems of one's own life is a luxury that comes at a price. The problems of the world are brought to our doorstep in their overwhelming entirety, and we are often incapacitated, rather than motivated, by the enormity of it all. The countless reported acts of violence breed fear, callousness, hopelessness, and obsession.

I am not saying the things reported in the newspaper don't happen, or that they should be ignored. I am saying that extraneous information just adds to the chaos, which is a high price to pay when one is seeking clear mind.

Does this mean you should eliminate newspapers from your life? Not necessarily. On impulse, you may pick up a newspaper because your intuition directs you to it, or you may read a newspaper for specific information. And, on occasion, you may read one for pure enjoyment—but drop the newspaper habit.

The most influential of the distractions we invite into our lives is probably television. We put our babies in front of the TV, and it entertains them. Preschoolers are taught by Sesame Street and kept entertained with cartoons. All kids know who "Big Bird" is, and Smurfs hold a special place in their affections. The television habit follows us through adolescence and into adulthood. Catchy sayings from commercials become part of our conversation.

The world of television merges with our reality. National surveys have shown time and again that, faced with a serious illness, people would trust the opinion of the actor who plays a famous doctor on their favorite day time drama series over that of their family doctor.

My older sister, Barbara, decided to deal with the issue of television in a very direct way. She had five children ranging from about three to twelve years of age. She felt the television was having a greater effect on her children than she wanted, and so made a rule that they could only watch it for one hour a week. They could choose the hour, but they had to agree on it among themselves. The choice was finally made to watch "Car 54 Where Are You?" and the show that followed it (this was about 1968). Her husband also enjoyed watching television occasionally, but it was generally late at night when the kids were asleep so it did not create a conflict.

On one occasion, as luck would have it, the family was visiting friends when TV hour approached. The children became agitated and began asking to go home (there was no television where they were). Their mother told them it wasn't appropriate to leave yet, and they would just have to watch during a different hour when they got home.

When they finally left, the children complained bitterly about how they had been made to miss "their" shows. The little one began to cry. As soon as they arrived home, Barbara strode quickly into the house and emerged carrying the TV set (quite a feat because TV's were heavier then, and she was only about 5'2" tall). She crossed the driveway, stood up on a low stone wall, and threw the set into the small canyon that ran behind the house. A few days later, her husband retrieved the smashed set and took it to the dump. The kids grew up without television.

It is important to understand that my sister was not angry with her children. She just felt the television encouraged a dependency that they didn't need, and she was a woman given to direct action.

Television provides us with a convenient escape from the reality of our lives, but at the same time we become involved in a milieu of fictional turmoil and distraction. If you are seeking the reality of the moment, you have no reason to escape. You experience unreasonable joy and so do not need distraction. Television, as a habit, is dropped.

At this point, I hope you are asking, "Is this fellow saying I have to take my TV to the dump and cancel the newspaper in order to lead a fulfilled life?" My answer is—I have no way of knowing what is required for you to experience fulfillment. The person seeking completeness is willing to do whatever is required. Do not fear silence and gladly let go of distraction and chaos. Experiment and trust your intuition to lead you toward your goal. Understand that in order to become focused, you must begin to drop the extraneous. One must stand apart from the chaos to be free.

Many of us are addicted to continual stimulation and cannot imagine life without it. If you are one of these, I can only assure you—there is life beyond chaos.

≈ 19 ≈

MEDITATION

The principal challenge to the person seeking completeness is to develop a mind that is clear, calm, alert, and
focused. The primary technique for achieving this goal
through discipline is meditation.

There are many types of meditation, any of which can
potentially give the desired result. The trick is to find the
technique, or combination of techniques, that is best
suited to you. Meditation in any form is a practice that
must be integrated into your life to be successful. If you
don't work towards discovering a technique you find
irresistible, you may drop the practice, and the end goal of
what I call "Clear Mind" may be lost.

The foundation of Zen Buddhism is meditative practice.
This practice is especially appropriate for developing the
attention of clear mind. A very brief description of one
technique is as follows: one adopts a cross-legged sitting
posture similar to the one that is used for statues of the

Buddha or that you see depicted in religious illustrations from India. The back is straight, and the head tilted down slightly, so that your eyes look at a point on the floor about four feet in front of you. You may close your eyes if you like. The hands are held in the lap with palms up. The left is placed on the right with the tips of the thumbs touching, so that together they form an oval. You feel relaxed but very solid, like an expert horseman who has supreme confidence in his mount and his ability to ride.

Now you begin to be aware of your breath. It enters without effort and you exhale slowly, letting it expand into the Universe. The breath enters again with no volition on your part, and you slowly exhale. As you continue this practice, focusing on awareness of the breath, you quickly discover the presence of an intruder. Your awareness of breath is continually intruded upon by thinking. The practice is to recognize each thought as being just a thought and returning your attention to the breath. This practice can be extremely frustrating as well as extremely rewarding, just as mastering any skill would be.

Meditation should be approached with both determination and humor. The emphasis should be in continuing the practice, not on achieving any particular result. The delight is in sitting quietly for a while. The goal of clear mind is simply a more balanced coexistence of intuitive and logical awareness. There are many books that give much more detailed instructions for meditation than presented here. Two of these are Meditation by Eknath Easwaran and The Three Pillars of Zen by Roshi Philip Kapleau. There are also many teachers that instruct in this practice.

A very useful discipline would be to do a sitting meditation of thirty minutes once or twice a day. However, once you get the idea, the essential part of meditation is to expand it into all of your daily activities. When you are driving down the freeway, you may suddenly become aware of your breathing. Focus your awareness on this. As you notice your breath, you are brought into the present moment. Soon you find that your breathing, which is always with you, is a key to bringing your awareness back to the present moment. Now you find that more and more often you are able to experience the moment directly. You are becoming a master of attention!

Instead of focusing on the breath, one can focus on a mantra. This is a word or phrase, often with a spiritual connotation, that you repeat silently in your mind. "Om" and "Mu" are mantras you could use. The meditation can be practiced in the same way as following the breath. Another variation is to repeat a prayer.

The thrust of all these meditations is to focus on something. As thinking arises it is recognized, and you return to your meditation. By doing this over and over, the mind is gently taught to pay attention. As one becomes adept at this practice, any thought begins to stand out sharply and clearly against the background of the meditation. This is quiet mind.

Some teachers insist on selecting a mantra suited to the particular student. When questioned about the significance of using a particular mantra, one teacher said, "You can repeat Coca-Cola for all I care. Just do it!" Some teachers believe that the different sound vibrations of different mantras have different effects on the student, while others find value in using words or phrases with religious connotations. Another commented that the value of charging a lot of money for receiving a "special" mantra and instruction in meditation is that the student then feels very committed and is excited by the hocus pocus. There is a lot of merit in this thought because classical meditation is essentially very boring at first, and it is difficult for most beginners to persevere.

These meditation techniques were developed in a different culture where people were not strangers to silence and what we consider to be discomfort was a way of life. It is almost impossible for most of us to sit quietly without feeling boredom so overwhelming as to be tantamount to panic. When doing sitting meditation, we are usually hoping desperately for some sort of spiritual vision to liven things up. To be told meditation is no more spiritual than anything else is not what we want to hear. The goal of spiritual attainment helps to keep us interested. We are a goal-oriented people and frequently need a sense of achievement to motivate us. If you just cannot make yourself do sitting meditation, don't despair! It's not for everyone.

Many things can work as meditation. For example, try walking meditation. Do a breathing meditation while walking on the beach, or in the woods, or downtown for that matter. Experiment until you find something that works. The best meditation for you at this time may be holding a state of attention while sitting on park benches or in coffeehouses—only you can tell. Remember—the goal is not to achieve pain but to achieve internal quiet and the ability to focus. If your resolve is strong, you will find the way to clear mind, or it will find you.

If your resolve is weak, you will try sitting meditation and, at the first sign of difficulty, decide "This is not for me!" Next you will try walking meditation, but your mind will wander and you will become discouraged. When no supernatural phenomenon occurs, you will think, "This stuff doesn't really work." Soon you will be back to your old ways, more certain than ever that there is no true joy in this life.

The strength of our resolve depends, for many of us, on how desperate we are. My purpose is to encourage you to strengthen resolve through discipline rather than desperation.

The goal of meditation is not pain, but some pain may need to be accommodated for learning to occur. Your resolve must be such that discomfort won't stop you as long as your intuition tells you to continue. The trick is to keep trying until you begin to feel the energy flow. Then you are hooked and there is no turning back.

Another type of meditation that most people associate with Zen training is sitting meditation with the koan. The best known koans are questions without an answer, such as "What is the sound of one hand clapping?" or "Who am I?" Other koans are more complicated riddles or paradoxical statements to be contemplated.

A very dedicated friend of mine was given a koan in the form of the task to "hear without thinking". He pursued this activity in his daily meditations for over a year. Finally, in desperation, he went before the Roshi (the Zen teacher) and said, "I have been trying for over a year to hear without thinking and I can't do it". The Roshi gave him a slightly puzzled look and said sympathetically, "Oh, well in that case, hear with thinking!"

This practice, at first blush, may sound somewhat perverse, silly, or, at the very least, unfathomable. What could possibly be achieved? This ancient technique certainly doesn't sound particularly applicable to life in our modern world. We can envision the benefits of sitting quietly with a mantra after a hectic day at work and a forty-minute bumper-to -bumper commute. How soothing! How spiritual! It is much more difficult to see the benefit of coming home and contemplating "Does a dog have Buddha nature?" for a couple of years.

I have never pursued formal koan training, however incidents in my life may have given me some insight into this odd practice. One of my first memories from kindergarten was being sent behind the piano for kissing the girl on the mat next to mine during "nap time".

As I look back, I see this as an almost ceremonial occasion on which I was first presented with the koan, "You want them all and you can't have them all; what can you do about it?"

Since I was a young man with a very strong sense of the Roman Catholic concept of sin, the koan was rephrased in a more pressing manner for my high school and college years as, "You want them all, and you can't have any of them". This thought became an obsession, as a good koan is wont to do.

When I married at age 22, the koan was rephrased slightly to, "You want them all, but you can only have one", which in some ways was worse than having none.

The marriage ended as I turned thirty. I moved to San Francisco determined to make up for lost time. Try as I might, the best I could do was to bring the koan to say, "You want them all, but you can only have some; what can you do about it?"

No matter what woman I was with, or how beautiful she was, there were always thousands more walking the streets, riding buses, shopping in stores, working in offices. I would see them and a piece of my heart would go out to them. There were so many wonderful, intriguing women I would never know. How unfair! What misery!

More years passed without any apparent progress. I still wanted them all. Love and a second marriage further complicated the situation. I would occasionally go traveling on my own in order not to feel confined by this relationship. I was often lonely and was attracted to many of the women I saw in my travels.

On one occasion, I was driving down the Oregon coast. The weather was gray, and my mood matched the weather. Would this torture never end? Would I ever outgrow this lust? What was I to do?

Suddenly, something swept over me. It was like seeing neon writing across the sky. It said, "That's right, you want them all and you can't have them all, Ha Ha Ha!"

I couldn't believe it, it was just a cosmic joke! All those years of internal turmoil were swept away. I was laughing and close to crying. Nothing had changed and yet everything was different!

Many years later I still want them all. So what? No problem, I can take a joke! The unanswerable has been answered: the paradox is just a paradox and no longer has any power over me.

My present understanding of koan practice, based on this and several similar incidents, is–a paradox is just a paradox and is only a problem to thinking mind. The mind chews on the paradox likes a dog with an old bone, until it finally has to give up. When it lets go, a different awareness can make itself known. You cannot think your way out of a koan, but if you persist you can experience resolution.

This practice can be incorporated into your life as a discipline that can lead to powerful insights. Formal koan practice is best pursued with a teacher, but informal practice is accessible to everyone.

To proceed, simply define the major unresolved issue in your life. Find a way to state the problem in one or two sentences. Repeat your statement of the problem to yourself frequently and keep looking for the answer. Part of the discipline is to view the problem as just a riddle and not get caught up in self-pity or remorse of any kind.

Once again, the main ingredient for success in using this technique for moving toward fulfillment is an unshakable resolve. Resolution can occur at any time, but we are generally not ready to accept the understanding that we seek. This is usually a matter of letting go of fears and preconceived notions about how things should be and embrace how things are. This may take years but so what? Be resolved to pursue completeness and be determined to enjoy the pursuit.

20

GOOD HEALTH

We are all familiar with the saying "Nothing matters as long as you have your health." This was the sort of thing my mother would say to lift our spirits after one of life's setbacks. The difficulty with this philosophy is that, at some point, most of us have to deal with poor health and face the challenge of experiencing completeness without good health. In fact, critical illness is a very effective vehicle for personal transformation. However, it has some obvious disadvantages, and opting to transform your life through good health, if you have a choice, can be just as effective (I use the term "good health" in the relative sense, meaning the best health you are capable of having at this time).

Physical fitness is certainly one of the keys to good mental and physical health. Exercise, for those who are able, is an excellent complement to meditation. Walking, running, cycling, swimming, weight training, or aerobics classes are all suitable for conditioning, depending on your fitness and preferences. Health clubs have proliferated in recent years, so equipment and instruction for all-around conditioning are available in most localities, and they suit the needs of many people. However, a health club is certainly not a requirement for exercising.

The benefits of physical exercise cannot be over-emphasized. The activity does not have to be strenuous, and age should not stop you. My father learned to ride a bicycle when he was 68 years old and rode almost daily, well into his seventies. This is an excellent low impact exercise, as long as you don't run into something. I have a 74-year-old friend who takes a brisk two-mile walk every morning. One of my aunts, a woman in her seventies, rides the bus to the end of the line and walks back. Her sisters work in the garden, which is their perfect physical fitness program. The main point, for our purposes, is that the body experience some fatigue. The amount of exercise required to achieve this will depend on you.

Eating is also an important part of health discipline. There are many books written about diet if you are inclined to research the subject. I have taken a moderate approach to diet–I use very little red meat, caffeine, alcohol, salt, or sugar. High fiber content and low fat seem to work for me. I feel better if I eat lightly and quit before I am full, although it is a real challenge.

Probably most important is to eat in a manner that you believe is healthy, and not to do anything else while you eat. Never read or watch television during meals. Instead, experience eating.

Good health is determined, at least in part, by our attitude toward health. A healthy attitude promotes a healthy outcome. Each morning we are presented with the opportunity to renew our lives and experience completeness.

No matter what we did yesterday, today is a new day, and we can be in harmony with the Universe if we so choose. The manner in which we start our day determines, to a large extent, whether or not we will take advantage of this opportunity for renewal. The early morning is a very special time of day, and a meditation or walk at this time seems to be especially beneficial.

Take advantage of this daily rebirth to experience the mystery of the Universe deliberately and with full attention. Reaffirm your commitment to experiencing the completeness of the moment and express appreciation for the good health that enhances this experience.

≈ 21 ≈

BECOMING
THE WARRIOR

The image of a warrior is often used as a metaphor for the person seeking to experience total fulfillment. This is a time honored and popular metaphor, since many of the disciplines used to resolve external battles also work toward the resolution of inner conflict. This warrior is not concerned with waging war but moving toward a meaningful life.

The essential elements of the warrior's life are resolve, responsibility, courage, daring, and discipline. The warrior's resolve is to experience completeness-in-the-moment. Warriors take responsibility for their lives and actions and never accept the roles of victims. They move into the unknown with courage and daring in order to experience completeness and introduce discipline into their lives to harness and utilize as much energy as possible in pursuit of this goal.

In Eastern traditions, the discipline of the martial arts has often been associated with spiritual training. The "hard style" martial arts are said to have their roots in the Shaolin Temple, a Buddhist monastery in China, where this type of training was first developed and practiced by the monks. These monks must have seen clearly the value of discipline in the battle for enlightenment.

The spiritual nature of this training has not been lost in modern times. A Vietnamese man, who took up martial arts at an early age, told me his teacher stressed that fighting was the lowest form of the martial arts.

"This training is about mastery—not fighting," he taught. "The warrior is striving to master himself."

Having mastered yourself, you can remain master in any situation. And, having mastered yourself, you no longer need to master any situation.

The warrior understands that this is a mysterious world in which we are surrounded by power.

The plight of the warrior coming in contact with power is similar to that of a man teaching himself to be a lion tamer when the only lions available are wild beasts that have just been captured. In order to learn, he must, at some point, enter the lion's cage. If he shows a lack of confidence, or any sign of fear, he will be ripped to shreds!

He trains carefully for the day when he will first step into the cage and face the lions. He begins to tighten up loose ends and depends on his impeccable life to see him through.

He understands that anything short of supreme confidence will result in a swift end, so he drops all thought of failure. Arrogance will distract him, so he cultivates respect. Anger will blind him, so he drops ego. Evil can overcome him, so he drops judgment. Laziness will make him slow, so he practices diligence. Fear will paralyze him, so he embodies love.

Like the lion tamer, you cannot afford to be sloppy in thought, speech, or actions. Weed self-doubt out of your consciousness by developing a positive attitude toward yourself and your surroundings. Observe your thoughts and let go of those born of fear, scarcity, and self-doubt—instead, focus on strength, abundance, and love. Begin to drop negative judgments and consider each situation as an opportunity for growth. In other words, actively reinforce the view of a supportive universe in which you play a harmonious and integrated role.

Of course, you do not know if the Universe is secure and supportive but choose to reinforce this view because it is the best alternative. You are preparing to engage power and wish to be at your best, and your best is when you feel at ease, in charge, and confident of success.

The disciplines discussed here are not those of the martial arts, but the essential elements are the same. Resolve, responsibility, courage, daring, and discipline are required to make one master of one's self.

Introducing discipline into one's life lets the Universe (and you) know that your intent is pure. It also puts "thinking mind" on notice that its days of running the show without restraint are over. You are ready to move ahead and are preparing to meet power.

Discipline, like most things, must be integrated into your life in a balanced manner in order to be effective. If you don't push yourself, your habits will remain the same and nothing really changes. If you are too aggressive, you become obsessed with the form of the exercise, and nothing is gained. The best approach is to train diligently but remain aware of the humor in the situation.

You are working very hard to gain something that is already yours—that is, this moment.

TRANSFORMATION

The first part of this book encourages a point of view that can bring about a transformation in your life. The promise is that there is a way of being in harmony with the moment so your actions are intuitively appropriate. The goal of transformation is to experience fulfillment, completeness, and guidance in your everyday activities.

The messages presented here point toward one avenue for transformation. However, transformation can come about in many ways. Many lives are transformed when people become so desperate that they are willing to let go of their view of the world. When this happens, they can embody a different kind of "knowing".

Critical or terminal illness, a serious car accident, and other near death experiences are events that often transform lives. When faced with impending death, we are sometimes willing to let go of our fears and judgments and live in the moment without resistance. While there

122

are many avenues to transformation, the underlying mechanism is generally a willingness to let go of our view of the world and "listen" or "surrender" to some "higher" power.

The spiritual warrior is determined to reach this state through discipline rather than desperation or some cataclysmic event. The advantages of the warrior's approach are obvious, in that attracting desperation and disaster into one's life is, at best, trying (although this seems to be a very common approach to learning).

Transformation is usually a gradual process with periods of great insight followed by periods during which the insights are digested and very little seems to be happening. These gestation periods are a natural part of the process and should not be cause for discouragement.

In some cases, one may have a more profound transcendental experience.

One friend, who did not follow any formal practice, spent a year walking around the city with no particular goal other than to experience and observe life. One day as he was sitting on a park bench, he noticed a humming sound and everything seemed to be outlined in a glow. As he looked around he had the very certain feeling that everything was exactly where and how it was supposed to be. This feeling slowly receded over the next few days but lingered for almost a month. He has since taken up a more formal meditation practice and the process of transformation continues. However, there is a lingering disappointment over the fact that this extraordinary experience has never been repeated.

While most seekers yearn for a powerful transcendental experience, it may cause more difficulties than it resolves.

These experiences often create a desire for more of the same and ordinary events pale by comparison. The resulting discontent with our everyday doings is just another stumbling block that must be overcome in order to experience true fulfillment.

Discipline provides a foundation for building a "new" life based on insight. The practice of various techniques to strengthen discipline gives the momentum that can move you through moments of uncertainty, frustration, fear, and revelation. Discipline also helps sustain humility and appreciation so you are not trapped as your ability to manipulate power matures.

The most important ingredient for success in transforming your life into one of fulfillment and unreasonable joy is resolve. The strength of your resolve may be determined by how desperate you are to find a solution to life's dilemmas. A desperate person has little to lose and may be willing to take steps that another would not. The problem with desperation is that it can lead to panic and poor judgment. The warrior's way is to work from strength rather than desperation.

The point of discipline is to train yourself to act in a certain way even though immediate rewards are not obvious. You motivate yourself with the promise of the ultimate reward of discovering completeness in-the-moment. This is, in a way, a trick you play on yourself, because you don't really know what "completeness-in-the moment" means or if it can be discovered. This trick allows you to continue to strengthen your life through discipline. At some point the life of discipline becomes its own reward, and there is no turning back. You begin to realize that the life of discipline is a life of attention, awareness, and joy and you are unwilling to go back to your old ways. You understand you are complete and have been all along. You begin to recognize your completeness in each moment.

If you choose to prepare yourself for transformation through discipline, you might proceed as follows. First, select a meditation technique that seems appropriate–for instance, following the breath. Set aside one or two thirty-minute periods a day for the practice. Return to this meditative attention during your daily activities as the opportunity arises. Introduce some sort of planned exercise at least every other day if you are physically able. Pay attention to eating and, as a minimum, follow the recommendations given above. Detach yourself from thoughts attached to fear and self-doubt and reinforce thoughts engendered by love and confidence. Let go of self-pity and commit yourself to accepting each situation that presents itself as an opportunity for further growth. Accept responsibility for your actions and let go of regrets and remorse. With these simple steps, you begin to take charge of your life and prepare to dance with power.

≈ part 3 ≈

DANCING
WITH POWER

Fly with wings of light,

Move without any sight.

Point in the direction

No one goes;

Learn, by leading,

What no one knows.

Everywhere we look we see evidence of powerful energies. The wind blows, rocks fall, and engines turn. Scientists spend a great deal of time observing and quantifying the effects of gravitational, electrical, magnetic and thermal forces. We observe these forces intimately, and they are so much a part of our lives, that we believe we understand them. In fact, based on past experience, we can predict how these forces affect the world around us, but we do not understand them. No matter how minutely we study, name, and quantify these forces, their fundamental nature is still mysterious and unknowable.

We are also surrounded by a vast "power" that is subtler in cause and effect. In our society, most scientists ignore this mysterious power. Psychologists conduct a small amount of research in the area of paranormal or psychic phenomenon, but the scientific community does not take this very seriously. The government does not, as far as I know, admit to sponsoring work in this area.* The energy that might be responsible for paranormal or "miraculous" phenomenon is mostly left for theologians to define, describe, and discuss in the context of religious ideology.

Mysterious power, whatever it is, has played a central role in our awareness for thousands of years. Christ was a miracle worker who is claimed to have changed water into wine, caused food to multiply, and even raised Lazarus from the dead. The history of miracles in the Christian faith does not stop with Christ. Large numbers of people visit Lourdes in France each year where crutches left behind by cured cripples line the walls.

Miraculous power is a cornerstone of many religions, to be called upon by the faithful through ritual or prayer. Personal access to this power was and is prevalent in aboriginal societies, where there are fewer other options for achieving one's goals.

If someone is running a high fever in our society, we give him or her antibiotics. To cover all the bases we might also pray for their quick return to health, but most of us are counting more heavily on the medical rather than the spiritual treatment. In aboriginal society it was quite the reverse. A shaman might administer a medicinal concoction, but the curing rite was primarily spiritual or magical in nature.

Despite our history of intimate relations with magical power, there are few people in modern society that truly believe we can perform miracles. Many people go to church every Sunday to pray and give thanks, but somehow they don't believe these rituals are a key to power. Most of us believe that miracles were a delusional phenomenon that ended with the Age of Reason.

My point is that we have two strongly conflicting views on miraculous power that exist concurrently in our society. On one hand, few people believe that miracles happen these days and are somewhat suspicious of the whole notion that they ever did. On the other hand, miracles are part of the very fabric of the religious beliefs that many of these same people espouse. Given this situation, some questions we might ask are:

(1)   Does miraculous power exist?

(2)   If it exists, can we manipulate it?

(3)   If the answers to the above questions are yes, then are there a "chosen" few for whom this power is available, or is it accessible to anyone?

(4)   How would one access this power?

(5)   How should this power be used?

I will answer these questions, to the best of my ability, as we go along.

Considerable information on government programs to exploit psychic phenomena for military and political purposes has become available since this was written. An article in Newsweek announced the CIA's admission that they had been using psychic spies for over 20 years. This apparently followed the program declassification in 1995. This was followed by a detailed account of government sponsorship of "psychic spy" programs in conjunction with Stanford Research Institute from the late sixties onward in Remote Viewers, the Secret History of America's Psychic Spies (1997) by Jim Schnabel. Mind Trek (1997) by Joe McMoneagle and Psychic Warrior (1998) are first hand accounts from the spies themselves.

≈ 23 ≈

MY INTRODUCTION TO POWER

I grew up a Catholic. The church of my boyhood was full of the mystery of Latin chants and a hierarchy of supernatural beings. The nuns told us many stories of miraculous happenings, often centered around appearances of the Virgin Mary, statues crying real tears, angels appearing to help people, miraculous healings, and similar themes.

My belief in these phenomena began to wane with the years. I knew the world was full of miracles and miraculous power because life was a miracle. Every tree, every blade of grass, every rock was a miracle beyond compare, each completely mysterious and unknowable. I accepted all of these "ordinary" miracles, but began to believe the extraordinary miracles were probably figments of someone's imagination. I kept asking, "Does miraculous power exist?" but had no idea how to find the answer.

It was at this time (the late sixties) I came across Carlos Casteneda's first book, The Teachings of Don Juan. This book spoke of our world as being both mysterious and magical. He talked about a power afoot in the world that was tapped by sorcerers to do their bidding. He also spoke of a "man of knowledge" as someone who had gone beyond sorcery to true wisdom. There was no way for me to assess the veracity of this description or to really understand what it meant, but it certainly appealed to me. Casteneda's tale of his apprenticeship excited me and inspired me to keep an open mind about such matters.

Then I met Pauline. A fellow worker had taken me to a lecture by a woman who she believed had psychic powers. I had looked forward with anticipation to the evening and envisioned a Gypsy woman performing feats of magic while avant-garde types nodded knowingly. Instead a neatly dressed grandmotherly woman in her mid-fifties with white hair and thick eyeglasses greeted me. She introduced herself as Pauline. Her audience was as respectable as a group of secretaries, electronics engineers, sales people, and accountants could be.

Pauline spoke of the power of the mind and how it can be used to work miracles. I was intrigued and decided to attend a seminar she taught to help people realize this potential. Pauline's basic teaching, as I understood it, was that it is within our power to have or do whatever we desire. The main requirements are to desire to have it, to believe you can have it, and that you deserve to have it.

The techniques Pauline taught were primarily the visualization techniques developed by Dr. Silvo, author of Mind Dynamics, but included other material she had gathered in a lifetime of spiritual pursuits. Her particular emphasis was to apply these techniques to spiritual healing.

The seminar was conducted on two successive weekends.

After the first weekend, many participants experienced fortuitous "coincidences" and insights that defied explanation. Stagnant lives suddenly became dynamic, despair turned to hope, and every one was very excited.

On the second weekend, each person was asked to write down the name and age of someone they knew well, but who would be unknown to the others taking the class. This information was then given to someone else, who was asked to describe the person named. Most of the descriptions were uncannily accurate. I was hooked.

I began to visit Pauline frequently, although my experiences raised more questions than answers. I tried to be a wholehearted participant but not a believer. I considered my involvement as an experiment and attempted to observe the outcome of this experiment in an unbiased manner. After attending Pauline's seminar workshops, my feeling was that something out of the ordinary was happening. Indications were that individuals could somehow cause extraordinary phenomena to occur; however, I did not understand the extent of the possibilities, how frequently the desired outcome was achieved, and the underlying rules for making these things happen.

One incident struck me as being particularly instructive. Pauline invited me to her house to meet Charles, another of her students. He was a computer engineer and worked for the same company as me, although we had never met. After introducing us she suggested that he do a psychic reading for me.

He closed his eyes, relaxed into a meditative state, and began making motions as though he were typing. Pauline explained that Charles was an atheist and didn't believe in psychic teachers or spirit guides, but he did visualize a psychic computer that gave him whatever information he needed.

After a few moments Charles commented that everything was in order and asked me if there was anything I would like to know.

"Describe my ex-wife and give me some insight into how to deal with her," I said. I was going through a difficult divorce and felt unreasonably persecuted. I was desperate for help.

"Give me here name, age, and tell me what city she lives in", Charles said.

"Her name is Elaine Natali, she's 32 and lives in San Francisco."

He made typing motions as though entering this data and suddenly looked very puzzled. "Something's wrong," he said, "the computer printout lists her age as 33." I was stunned–her birthday had occurred the week before and, as usual, I had forgotten it!

Once this was cleared up, his "computer" printed out a very accurate description of her psychological make-up and gave me valuable insight into her motivation.

This incident strengthened my conviction that something was occurring which was outside of the realm of possibilities as described by conventional science. Further, the power to perform these feats was being tapped by "serious" individuals with a scientific background. In addition, a belief in "God" or some other dogmatic description of the Universe was not a requirement for tapping this power. Charles also was an example of someone who learned to access this power through training as opposed to being a "born psychic".

Over a period of time, I met a number of engineers,

physicists, and medical doctors who studied under Pauline. These people usually started out as skeptics, but soon became convinced they too could perform "miracles". They participated as practitioners who wanted to use this power to enhance their lives, not as scientific observers who wanted to study the phenomenon.

I personally tried to participate fully without becoming a believer or a disbeliever. I was especially interested in the interpretations and explanations participants would formulate around these practices. Metaphysical visions of "spirit guides" and "teachers" were frequently described. The presence of Christ and other masters was noted. The voices of "ascended Tibetan masters" were "channeled" through people. Terms such as "higher self" and "past reincarnation" were heard frequently.

I do not argue with the authenticity of any of these manifestations or explanations but consider them to be interpretations of the nameless power. They strike me as Thinking Mind's attempt to give form to the formless. The power of the Universe seems to be willing to adopt any form with which one is comfortable. I expect that if we were meditating with a group of American Plains Indians, we would have been visited by the "Woman of the North Wind," the "Spirit of the Badger," or some other form that would make sense in a culture closer to nature than our own.

One night, Jeanette, an energetic grandmother who worked in the same office as me, attended one of Pauline's lectures. After the lecture, she went up to Pauline and said, " I have one leg shorter than the other and have had to wear a shoe with an inch-high lift since I was a little girl. If I go without it even for a short time, I get a terrible headache. Can you fix it?"

"Of course!" Pauline replied.

"Oh nooo," my inner voice cried, "this is crazy. After this debacle I won't dare show my face around work!"

What would people at work say when they heard about Pauline's wild claims and her failure to produce a cure? Developing the power of your mind was one thing, but hanging around with deluded people was another. They would think I was either very gullible or just plain nuts.

Pauline told Jeanette to lie on the floor. The group of about twenty people attending gathered around while Pauline adjusted Jeanette into position on her stomach. I stood by, mentally wringing my hands as Pauline removed Jeanette's shoes and put her heels together.

Indeed, one leg appeared to be about an inch shorter than the other leg. Pauline raised the short leg until the foot was about 18 inches off the floor and held it for a moment. She lowered it and the heels were perfectly aligned. She commanded Jeanette to stand up. Jeanette stood and then dropped to her knees sobbing and shouting, "Thank you Jesus! Thank you Jesus!" She was cured.

An emotional scene ensued. Those of us watching were in shock—we had witnessed a "miracle".

I finally got Pauline off to the side and asked her how she did it. "I simply visualized her leg growing the inch necessary to make her legs equal" she replied casually.

Jeanette experienced whatever happened as the "power of Christ". Pauline didn't seem to mind and gave thanks that the Power was able to work through her. The Power didn't seem to mind Jeanette's interpretation—she left in her bare feet, carrying her shoes.

Jeanette never wore a lift again in the time I knew her. I left that job about three years later.

I cannot swear to the authenticity of this "miraculous" cure. There are too many subjective elements in a situation like this to be absolutely certain what happened; however, it is the sort of thing that gets your attention.

Both Pauline and Jeanette were powerful women with a deep spiritual faith. To them there was nothing "impossible" about what happened, and that, in the end, might be the determining factor as to what is possible.

A week or two after Jeanette's leg "grew", some friends stopped to visit my wife and me on a Saturday afternoon. I retold the story of the miraculous cure with considerable relish. Marie, a woman in her early twenties with a devilish air, began to grin. "I have one arm shorter than the other. I have to shorten all my blouses three-fourths of an inch on the right arm, can you fix it?"

I hesitated–"I don't think so."

My wife, who had not said anything to this point, made it very clear that, in her opinion, I should not fool around with such things.

Marie had recently left the convent because she felt that, while devout, her true calling was not that of a nun. She explained that in the convent all of her "habits" had to be shortened to accommodate the difference in her arm lengths. This, of course, reopened the discussion of whether we should attempt a "cure". My wife, uncharacteristically, suggested quite forcefully that I forget the whole subject.

Naturally, there was no way that I was really going to pass up this golden opportunity for an experiment. Obviously it wouldn't work, and since we were among friends, it would make for a good joke, mostly on me.

After considerable hesitation on both sides, Marie and I reached a joint agreement to try to grow her arm. My wife, who seldom worries about things, made it known again that she didn't think this was a good idea. Her reticence didn't even slow me down.

I told Marie to hold her arms in front of her. I took the short arm and raised it to the vertical position. I then brought it down while doing my visualization but immediately raised it again and did the whole process once more "for good measure".

When I lowered her arm the second time, an odd feeling crept over me as the two arms became parallel. The previously short arm was now three-fourths of an inch too long! Pandemonium broke out. Marie began to cry hysterically and I, in spite of myself, was laughing uncontrollably!

A voice in my head was saying, "Oh, ye of little faith!" I had done twice what a wiser man would have known only needed to be done once. This was the ultimate cosmic joke.

I tried to calm Marie by telling her I would grow the other arm to match the one that had grown too long. This was the wrong thing to say and brought another onslaught of tears.

Meanwhile my wife, who has a cool head in an emergency, had gotten on the telephone and handed it to me. I heard Pauline's voice ask, "What have you done?" I told her, along with some rather lame apologies.

"Tell that broad to be quiet!" she commanded (Pauline knew how to take charge). When order was restored, she said, "Have her put her arms above her head.....Now, everyone think equalization". And then, "Okay, tell her to bring her arms down until they are stretched out in front of her". The arms were just right.

This incident occurred about sixteen years ago. I have seen Marie only three times since then, the last time being just a few months ago. She is happily married and teaches school. She assured me that her arm grew and that her arms have remained of equal length ever since.

I continued to participate in metaphysical meetings and witnessed a variety of phenomena. I found it intriguing and, at times, exciting. However, I noticed that more and more frequently my wife, who generally went with me, found various reasons why she could not attend. It finally became obvious she no longer cared to be involved in these meetings, and I asked her for an explanation. She commented that while all of the unexplainable phenomena were interesting, they were also very distracting. She felt she wanted to pay attention to her "ordinary" life and get that in order before seeking extraordinary experiences. The wisdom of her approach was clear. It was obvious to me that I also had much work to do towards appreciating my everyday world, and so I too withdrew from the meetings.

Not long after that we moved from the area and contact with Pauline became very infrequent for several years. However, I have recently visited Pauline and her husband several times and am happy to say that the experience is as refreshing and rewarding as ever. Now in her mid-seventies, she still rises early to do her morning chants and prayers on the patio. She does not appear to have aged much, and her cooking is better than ever. She remains an inspiration to myself and her other friends.

The events I have described may or may not seem unusual to you, depending on your past experience. I gather they may not be as unusual as one might think, although such extraordinary events are isolated experiences for most of us. Many people are reluctant to discuss such experiences, partly because they are not generally accepted in our society, but also because we tend to doubt our own observations.

My introduction to power led me to some preliminary conclusions. First, I concluded that "miraculous power" does exist and can be manipulated. Second, this power is apparently available to everyone, although not necessarily in equal measure. My observation is that some people become adept at accessing this power much more readily than others. Further, we seem to have individual charac-teristics that lead to different "talents" when working with power. One person may show a talent for clairvoyance, while another might heal by "laying on of hands", and a third might "channel" esoteric knowledge. It further appears that a truly "clear channel" is rare indeed and success in manipulating power is sporadic.

I have given you a glimpse of my introduction to power as a means of stimulating your memory of similar events in your own life or at least piquing your curiosity. Now, in case this is unfamiliar territory, let me attempt to intro-duce you to power.

≈ 24 ≈

ACCESS
TO POWER

The secret to accessing and directing miraculous power is so simple that, if you don't know it already, you won't believe it when I tell you. It is this: power is directed by your thoughts! It is as simple as that. Am I one of the few who knows the secret? Not at all. Most book stores (at least in California) have somewhere between ten and three hundred books that say the same thing. A few examples are: You Can Work Your Own Miracles by Napoleon Hill (a protégé of Andrew Carnegie), How To Have More In A Have Not World by Terry Cole-Whittaker, The Ultimate Secret To Getting Absolutely Everything You Want by Mike Hernacki, and Personal Power Through Awareness by Sonaya Roman. All of these books (and they are only a few of many) reveal in one way or another the secret I have stated. As a matter of fact, this principal hardly qualifies as a secret when it is so widely discussed.

If tapping this energy is so simple, why isn't everyone

doing it? Well they are, but in order to be a "clear chan-nel" one must be capable of holding a focus. Most people live in distraction and chaos, so their thoughts attract little power. Maybe you have noticed that successful people generally are quite single-minded in their endeav-ors and have a clear image of what they consider a success.

By holding a goal clearly in mind, energy is somehow set in motion to help you achieve this goal. If you are dis-tracted, the motion is stopped. If you perceive failure, the motion is reversed!

The secret is focus. Focused thought directs power and power makes the thought a reality. It is important to make a distinction here between "thinking" and "thought". Thinking about something has little influence; it is holding a thought or visualizing a result that is powerful.

Talking about our relationship to creative power is diffi-cult, since we are trying to describe the indescribable. We can, however, postulate simple models that relate cause and effect based on our experience. The objective is not to be academic but to find practical means for working with the mystery around us.

When I was a kid, my friends and I would while away summer afternoons by placing leaves or bits of paper on the sidewalk and trying to ignite them from the sun's rays focused with a small magnifying glass. We usually had little plastic lenses that we got as a prize in Crackerjacks or a cereal box. These lenses were clouded and scratched from living in our pockets, and it was a real challenge to start a fire with one of them.

One day a friend sneaked out with his grandfather's good reading glass. It was a lens about three inches in diameter and of good quality. That lens was capable of focusing a lot of the sun's energy on a very small spot and could start a fire in no time. It was very impressive.

In a way, our mind is like the magnifying glass. We can think of it as focusing power on a particular result. If it is cloudy with distraction, creative power is not focused effectively and not much happens. Someone with a clear, quiet mind can focus power very effectively and miracles happen.

A very imprecise description of the situation is something like this: each of our thoughts or feelings attracts some power to make that thought become a reality. The amount of power a thought commands depends on the clarity of the mind holding the thought. The reality we experience is determined, in some measure, by the "average" of these thoughts. We must keep in mind that this model is only an attempt to approximate, in a simple fashion, how things really work. While not overly elegant, it will serve as a start for discussion purposes.

Let's assume, for the moment, that this description has some validity and see what it implies. First, we might note that disciplines to reduce chaos and develop a clear, calm mind would be very useful for directing power. We also remember that power is directed toward "manifesting" the thoughts we hold in our mind, so it would be wise not to entertain negative thoughts. We would infer that as a person achieves clear mind through discipline, he or she must develop a positive attitude in order to survive. That is, as the ability to focus power increases, one must be careful where it is focused.

How can we determine if this description is valid? Well, if it is true, then there must be examples in the world around us to support this point of view. We certainly know that the mental images we hold have an important influence on our health and sense of well being, but do they really focus power? Let me give a few examples.

I have a friend who is president of a company he started with two partners. The company presently grosses about eighty million dollars a year and is still growing. One day, during lunch, the conversation turned to the subject of leading a successful life. My friend said there was indeed a "secret" to success he would like to share, but it was so simple that it was difficult to state in a way that would make an impression. He said, "It's a little like wearing rose colored glasses. You have to have a goal in mind and no matter what disasters occur, you assume they are somehow opportunities in disguise and keep working toward your goal."

Now I'll admit this doesn't sound very profound, and that is part of the problem. It is just too simple to get anyone's attention. However, you can see that some very successful people believe that focusing thoughts on a particular result and not becoming distracted is one of the keys to success. That is, they focus on an image of success and success comes to them. Of course, it is not quite as simple as that. Focusing on success will "attract" opportunities to you that can lead to your goal, but you must act on those opportunities.

We might ask if this success is just a case of hard work and intelligence. The fact is the world is full of hard working, intelligent people, but very few of them feel they are really successful. Of course, it might just be luck that some are more successful than others. In fact, "luck" is exactly what we attract when we hold an image of success. I maintain the difference is the clarity of the vision, the ability to focus, and the courage to act on intuitive messages.

Not long ago, I presented these ideas to a colleague for whom they were entirely foreign. When I was finished, he said it brought to mind an experience that had mystified him for some time.

A few years previously he had decided to buy some land to build a house. Unfortunately, his resources were limited, and the properties he liked were out of his price range. Rather than give up, he began driving around the countryside looking for pieces of property that he liked. When he saw a site he liked, he noted its location and added it to a list he kept. When he had several sites on the list, he went to the County Assessor's office and got the names of the owners, hoping to find someone who would sell him a suitable site at a price he could afford.

He saw one parcel of land that was his dream site but knew it was worth much more than he could pay. He called the owner anyway, figuring he had nothing to lose. A woman answered and when he asked if she would consider selling the property, she said, "I think so, give me your number and I'll call you back". He complied, but assumed he would never hear from her.

Fifteen minutes later she called back and said, "I've just talked to my husband, and we've agreed to sell you the property for what it cost us eight years ago. If you don't have the cash, we will work out payments. You can consider the property yours and there is no hurry about the paperwork; however, if you want this in writing you can drop by. I would be interested in meeting you." He, of course, could not believe what he was hearing! This land was in a desirable part of California and land prices had tripled in eight years!

He immediately raced over to the owner's house to get her signature before she changed her mind. When he got there, the lady was very cordial and seemed to be some what amused. She said, "I have a story to tell you about how I happen to own this property. Eight years ago I was taking a drive in the hills and saw a 'For Sale' sign. A voice inside me said, 'Buy this property.' I have owned it ever since but never knew why. Yesterday my inner voice said, 'Sell.' I've been hanging around the house today expecting a call." The woman continued on to say that she was going to give some of the money to a friend who had always wanted to take a trip to Hawaii.

Shocked by her carefree attitude toward money, my friend mumbled something about her "amazing generosity".

"I never worry about money. The world always seems to give me whatever I need," she said.

How did the Universe arrange all of this? I have no idea, but it clearly illustrates power at work.

Power is always available to us and is a vital ingredient of life for those who have a natural ability to focus and a clear goal in mind. Training and discipline can heighten these abilities and the possibilities of precipitating extraordinary events such as "miracle cures" is open to us. I have had the experience of channeling this power, and so I am convinced that it exists. If you are not convinced, you may want to experiment. I suggest you start slowly. One exercise that turns out to be both amusing and amazing is this: next time you are driving to a place where it is difficult to find parking, visualize an empty parking space close to where you are going. Remember you don't have to believe anything, just act as though you believe it. The results may surprise you.

When you are ready to try something a bit more complex, try this. Sit in a meditative position, or lie down on your back. Close your eyes and relax deeply. When you feel your body is very heavy and still, visualize a result you desire. For example, suppose you wish to sell your car. You see yourself standing in the driveway holding the money someone has just given you. The happy new owner is driving your car away. You can feel the relief of having the car sold. You have just set in motion movement in the Universe towards making your visualized result a reality. Now go about doing whatever you would normally do to sell your car, knowing that the right customer is being attracted to you. Since all thoughts tap power, any negative thoughts you have regarding the possibility of a sale will countermand your original order.

As with any skill, one should attempt small successes before big ones. Matching a task to the student's ability is important. If the task is too easy, the student becomes bored and quits. If the task is too difficult, the student does not make any progress and becomes discouraged.

I have known people who, after some modest initial successes with power, immediately started visualizing themselves receiving a million dollars. These endeavors have not been successful, and they have become disillusioned. Their approach is similar to a beginning piano student thinking he is ready to play a Beethoven sonata because he has mastered "Twinkle, Twinkle Little Star". Most people do not have the "power" or clarity of focus to draw a million dollars to themselves in a short time. In fact, by attempting it they often make their financial situation worse. This is because their wish usually reflects the fact that they feel they don't have enough money. The Universe attempts to arrange the external experience to match your thoughts and feelings. If your thoughts are focused on not having enough, you will generally attract experiences that confirm you don't have enough.

Several of my friends and acquaintances are millionaires. Few of them got rich by just visualizing a lot of money (although this may not be out of the question for a powerful person). Most of them have held an image of monetary success for many years. They generally are not afraid to act on their own opinions or intuition, even if some risk is involved. Their underlying orientation is one of having more rather than not having enough. The image of success appears to feed on itself and attracts more success. That is, as the image on which they are focused becomes clearer and better defined, it is confirmed more strongly by the world around them. This does not mean these people feel happy, complete, or fulfilled, although they may. They are focused on financial success and it is drawn to them. This is how power works.

A friend of mine, who has achieved amazing things in his life, has had to face what sometimes seemed to be impossible tasks. When asked how he approached these tasks he replied, "Little steps for little feet". I recommend this approach when experimenting with power. I further recommend you finish reading this book before you attempt any serious wizardry.

POWER – FRIEND
OR FOE?

Once we see the results of consciously focusing power, we are hooked. Our childhood dream has come true–we have found Aladdin's Lamp! Fame and fortune await us, why hold back?

Most religions recognize the power of prayer (focused mind). Christian history is replete with miraculous events–Christian "saints" are credited with miracles and evangelists claim miraculous healings. Gurus from India are reported to have miraculous phenomena occur in their presence.

But, a word of caution; Don Juan told Carlos Castaneda that "power" was the Man of Knowledge's third natural enemy (after fear and clarity). The Zen tradition also gives us subtle warnings and miracles are seldom mentioned. Why are the Zen masters so silent? Is it because they lack the power to perform miracles?

A story is told of two Zen monks of considerable attainment who set out on a journey together. After walking some distance they came to a deep river that had to be crossed. The ferryman's hut was on the other side of the river, but their shouting for him was of no avail. He was apparently not at home. One monk, after looking around to make sure no one was coming along the trail, said, "Come on, let's cross," and started walking on top of the water! He looked back and saw his companion was still standing on the bank.

"Aren't you coming?" he called.

"Who would travel with someone that is in such a hurry?" the other monk replied as he lay down to nap in the sun.

We may judge from this story that the silence of the Zen tradition on miracles is deliberate and not a product of ignorance, disbelief, or lack of power. Instead, the impression is that miracles are best treated with an amused tolerance. But why? Is it because power can be obsessive and become a goal in itself? Maybe it is a lot like money. For someone obsessed with money, there is never enough of it. King Midas wished everything he touched would turn to gold. When his wish came true, he quickly found it wasn't a very good idea!

Someone obsessed with power will never feel powerful enough. Continually looking for the next miracle, one can't see the miraculous surroundings. They live in continual distress and are starving in a Garden of Eden. Power, as an end in itself, is not useful because it, like money, can never satisfy our inner need.

In relating how I was introduced to power, I stated that I witnessed and participated in several situations in which "miracles" seemingly occurred. These were, to me, very exciting and even spectacular occurrences. I am still surprised that I had the good sense (with the help of my wife's insight) to step back from attempting to create more "miracles". I avoided obsession.

I will call someone who devotes him or herself to manipulating power a "sorcerer". The term sorcerer contains no moral judgment for better or worse; it just means one whose goal is to focus miraculous power effectively.

It is evident that many of the disciplines of the "spiritual warrior" would also be useful training for the sorcerer. However, while the sorcerer may choose to become the warrior, the warrior, who is seeking completeness, must move beyond sorcery. The warrior's goal is not to manipulate power but to experience his or her own completeness in the moment.

The warrior's concern is not what is possible but what is appropriate. Power becomes an ally in making the appropriate a reality regardless of the possibilities.

If someone becomes obsessed with power before achieving the insight of "appropriate action", their only alternative is to direct power with "thinking mind". This is like giving a loaded gun to a spoiled child. Thinking mind thrives on making impossible demands, and you have no idea where power will be focused next. This is not the path to fulfillment and inner peace.

I remember several variations on a childhood fairy tale about someone being granted three wishes and the last wish was always, "I wish to be back in my own home with everything the way it was before this started". The point is, power is of no use without the "wisdom of appropriateness".

The value of discipline now becomes clearer. The disciplined person, through mastery, is able to meet power with restraint. The goal is clear, and they are not seduced by power's siren song of control over the world around them. They know that without wisdom, power is useless. They view power much as one would view a high spirited and powerful horse. When the master horseman mounts, the horse takes him to his destination swiftly and surely, but woe be to the novice who brashly attempts to ride this horse!

At this point you might question why, if power is such a problem, I brought the subject up at all. The answer is I had no choice. Distraction and chaos act as an umbrella that normally isolates us from power. As we learn to quiet the prattling of our inner voice, the umbrella is pierced, and we begin to experience power in our lives. To understand clearly that power is not our goal cannot be an excuse for avoiding it, if one is to experience completeness.

A powerful person taking a "holy vow" of nonviolence is a strong action. A weak person taking a "holy vow" of nonviolence is beside the point. The spiritual warrior appreciates the necessity of meeting and using power. It is neither friend nor enemy, but an ally she controls with mastery. Power is the warrior's legacy, and she greets it with both joy and restraint.

≈ 26 ≈

APPROPRIATE
ACTION

The concept of obtaining guidance from a "higher" source is certainly not a new one. People pray for guidance all the time. Our dollar bill proclaims, "In God we trust." Politicians croon "May God give us the wisdom ....."

When I was a child, the Catholic nuns taught us that everyone has a "guardian angel" who guides us and warns of danger. The Plains Indians went on vision quests in search of a spirit power that would give them guidance. People who take the metaphysical approach to spiritual learning often have a "spirit guide" that comes to give them guidance when they are meditating. J. Z. Knight "channels" the esoteric New Age guidance of the unseen entity Ramtha for audiences that include film stars.

Explorers and adventurers who undertake journeys of extended duration and physical hardship often have experiences of a "presence" that guides them. Joshua Slocum, the first man to sail around the world single-handed, had, when he became ill from food poisoning, the experience (or delusion) of having his boat sailed all night through a stormy sea by the phantom pilot of Columbus's ship the Pinta. A commercial salmon fisherman, who fished small boatsfrom California to Alaska, told me, "knowledge alone is not enough to survive. You have to have a "sixth sense" to warn you of danger." A long-time law enforcement officer told me the same thing.

I was always open minded, but undecided, on the question of "divine guidance" until I received some myself. The birth of our first child, when I was in my mid-thirties, was a traumatic event for me. I resented the additional responsibility and financial burden that a new baby represented, especially since my career held no enjoyment or meaning for me.

When the baby was about a year-and-a-half old, I decided to take a break. I loaded my camping gear into my pickup and headed north. My wife was probably relieved to see me go–I had been depressed and withdrawn for most of the time since she became pregnant. I left my truck in British Columbia, tossed my sleeping bag, tent and other essentials into my backpack, and boarded the ferry for Alaska. I met people easily and was soon making friends–travelling from one small town to another, sleeping on couches , helping with chores, and seeing the sights.

My "old" life and concerns quickly faded . I avoided thinking about the "past" because I didn't want to deal with it (as Zorba said, "house, wife, kids–the whole catastrophe"), and I couldn't even begin to imagine the future, so I began to live entirely in the present. My anxiety slipped away and life unfolded effortlessly.

Early one morning, after an all night ride from Ketchikan to Prince Rupert, I felt something urging me to return to the ferry dock and get on the ship going South (an overnight trip)–something I had no desire to do. I had never experienced strong inner "guidance" before, but the command was compelling, and I did what I was told.

As I boarded the ferry I muttered, "this had better be good because I don't want to do this". I began strolling the decks wondering why I was there when I saw an exotic woman leaning against the railing. Overcoming my shyness, I mumbled some inanity to her and we struck up a conversation.

It didn't take me long to realize that I had been "guided" to the woman of my dreams. I had always been attracted by Oriental women (although I didn't know any), but in this case the combination of a Chinese father and an English mother had produced a woman that pushed addictive buttons I didn't even know I had. She looked Asian, with long black hair that hung to her waist, but was uncharacteristically large breasted (she later joked, "That's my English half").

Kim had grown up in Vancouver, B.C. and understood city ways, but had chosen to teach elementary school in isolated Native villages along the Nass River, where transportation was by boat, airplane, or, in the winter, walking on the frozen river. She told me, "In Vancouver, knowing what's in fashion and what restaurants are "in" is important information. On the Nass, survival depends on knowing where the holes in the ice are when you're walking on the river."

I was fascinated. My primary reason for travelling in the North was that I had a consuming interest in Native art and culture. Finally I had met someone who was involved in what for me was the ultimate adventure. We struck a responsive chord in each other, and quickly became inseperable. We spent time together in Vancouver and then went camping "up island." It soon became clear to me that I wanted to spend the rest of my life with her.

Of course, my convenient amnesia did not change the fact that I was married and had a daughter. I called my wife every few days and was evasive (in a cowardly way) about why I kept extending my stay. Finally it became impossible to put my return off any longer and I prepared to drive back down the coast to Santa Cruz. Kim's position was, "You have a woman and a daughter—go back and see if you can make that relationship work. If you can't, I'll come and live with you."

There was no doubt in my mind that I had to be with Kim. It was divinely ordained—after all, I had been given specific directions by an unseen power to get on the ship that day in order to meet her (it was, by the way, the first time she had ever ridden that ferry boat). I dreaded facing my wife and going through the divorce, but I couldn't wait to be living with Kim in the total bliss I knew was waiting for us.

Driving down the rainy coast, I alternated between remembering each precious moment with Kim, and imagining the dreaded confrontation with my wife. Suddenly, in the midst of my chaotic thoughts, I experienced a moment of profound silence and a voice in my head said, "It's not a question of whether or not you want a daughter, you have a daughter." In that instant, I underwent a fundamental conversion. I understood instantly what was being said—if I turned my back on my responsibility, I would just create the situation again and again until I dealt with it (Kim already thought she might be pregnant) and in the meantime, a string of fatherless children would be left behind. I was shaken and vowed, without hesitation, to take full responsibility for my daughter.

But now I was left with the quandry of what to do about the marrage. I had always been attracted to women and had on several occasions been unfaithful, although I was seldom honest about it. Now the whole issue seemed overwhelming (even though I was madly in love with Kim)–I wanted them all and couldn't have them all. As I've already told you, the voice, as if reading my mind, said, "That's right, you want them all, and you can't have them all, Ha Ha Ha!" Once again, I had no trouble understanding the message–that's just the way it is, and in this case, the joke's on me.

"Okay, I can take a joke, but what about monogamy?"

"Instead of trying to discover a little bit of the miracle in a lot of women, why don't you try to discover all of the miracles in one woman? That could take you a lifetime."

"Ohhh, I see what you are saying . . . but I have a problem that you can't help me with."

"Give us a try."

"I don't love my wife."

"Hey! If you can love a stranger, you can love a friend."

Things seemed to break loose inside me. I "saw" how I had opened up to Kim, a woman I had only known for three weeks, and how it was possible to do the same with Linda, who had always been a friend to me.

I arrived in Santa Cruz a converted man. In the meantime our cabin, which we had put up for sale before I left, had sold, and Linda had moved in with her folks. I had been gone for four months–she assumed the marrage was over and was not interested in continuing it. However,

157

after much pleading she relented. I immediately began to see the miracle in every bit of her, starting with her elbows. I was soon madly in love with both my wife and daughter.

I phoned Kim and in her generous way she accepted the situation as the best possible outcome. She wrote me a note a few years later to let me know that she was doing well and was about to be married.

Years later I am still in awe of how I was lead through a series of experiences that resolved things I thought could never be resolved. It is not lost on me that much of what I did was "sinful" and "dishonest". The Universe did not seem to judge me, but rather worked with what was at hand to show me a greater truth. I am left with the following conclusions: the Universe is not a machine; help is available; we better have a sense of humor, because It does.

After my "conversion," I began to seek guidance whenever I faced new difficulties. I noticed I received the strongest intuitive "feelings" when my life was most out of control. It finally occurred to me that I could avoid some of the pain and stress in my life if I tried to hear this "voice" before a crisis occured.

I began listening for the intuitive voice when times were good and felt I was having some success, but there was certainly no way to prove it, even to myself. Over the years a pattern developed. If I had a certain goal in mind, a "coincidence" would occur that provided an opportunity to move toward that goal. If I seized the opportunity, before long another coincidence would occur. I decided to act on opportunities even if I didn't see how they were related to my goal. Often it would seem that I wasn't getting anywhere, and then suddenly my goal was achieved!

The process works something like this. Suppose you are seeking your fortune but don't know where to find it. One day you walk into a used book store on an impulse. As you are browsing, you open an old book and a piece of paper falls out. It is a hand-drawn map of a nearby area with directions to dig under a certain old tree. You are certain your dreams have come true and that you have found an authentic treasure map. You try to be nonchalant as you purchase the book and hurry out of the store. You get digging tools and proceed to follow the map. You find the tree and soon uncover a bottle with a note and a key in it. The note says to go to locker No. 12 in the Greyhound bus station and open it with the key.

You get over your initial disappointment of not finding the treasure and you race over to the bus station, certain you will be rich in a few minutes. When you get there, you open the locker and find a bus ticket to a town about 60 miles away with a note telling you to go to a certain tavern in that town and ask the bartender for the suitcase Joe Smith left for safekeeping.

As you may have guessed, the suitcase contains further directions, and the story continues until you have given up all hope of finding the treasure. However, you have been following the treasure hunt clues for so long that you continue on the search without expectations of reward, because it has become a way of life. And then one day you find the treasure.

This story illustrates the first rule of power, which is: As you visualize a goal clearly, the Universe moves to accommodate that result—in some cases the outcome is swift, but in most, a journey must be embarked upon to reach your goal. Once this motion is initiated, amazing "coincidences" occur and unusual opportunities present themselves. This is power in action. "Clues" point the way, intuitive insights arise, and a path unfolds. The process appears to be orchestrated by an unseen hand, which I perceive as "guidance."

As you follow the path, act on the clues, and seize the opportunities, you move toward your goal.

Now we come to the second rule of power, which is: you must be willing to act on whatever clues you are given. It may mean quitting a job, selling a car, reading a particular book, or just changing your point of view. Act in spite of fear and take full responsibility for the consequences.

In my experience, the guidance received never requires action beyond what one is capable of at the time. The Universe seems to accommodate the "small steps for small feet " rule. If you start out weak, you will be guided until you are strong. As a result, the novice generally takes much longer to reach a goal than the master.

As you follow the path of appropriate action, the beauty of the process unfolds. As you look back, you see that what appeared to be random meanderings in fact took you to places that you needed to visit before you were ready for the next part of the journey. Around each bend in the road new insight awaits. The path is uniquely tailored to you.

Will this process still work if you put limitations on what you are willing to do? Of course, after all, we are all limited. Limitations act like roadblocks and leave fewer avenues open for the accomplishment of your particular goal. This process is, in fact, perfectly suited to help us overcome our limitations.

Celeste, a massage therapist, had the intuitive perception that she should go to India and meditate with a particular guru. Going would require that she give up her lucrative practice as well as a lovely, but inexpensive, apartment. The trip would put her in a precarious financial position and seemed totally impractical. However, she decided to go anyway.

Once the decision was made, events fell into place so that the trip became a reality. Her experiences in India brought her to a new level of awareness, and she was very happy she had followed the prodding of her "inner voice."

Suppose, however, that she had not been able to overcome her fears and decided against making this journey. Would she still be able to progress toward her goal of greater understanding? Of course, as long as her intention remained clear. In this case, the Universe might present less frightening alternatives by which she could pursue her path. Progress would be slow until she gained the under-standing necessary to overcome her self-imposed limita-tions and take more direct action. Unfortunately, once your intention has set energy in motion, the slower path is not always easier—just slower.

The Universe is, by nature, creative and imaginative. It will respond to your intentions as appropriate and present you with circumstances that allow you to move toward your goal. This is a subtle process based on the rule, "Experience is the best teacher." You are given the oppor-tunity to face and overcome those fears which stop you from moving forward.

We are often capable of taking much larger steps than are comfortable for us but choose to live well below our potential rather than take the risks necessary to achieve our goals. However, once your intention is clear, the Universe will find ways to spur you on. For some of us, change is so uncomfortable that we must be driven to the limits of desperation and despair before we are willing to let go and move onward.

My own experience has been that I was much more willing to take strong action out of desperation than out of a "disciplined willingness." The Universe has been quick to accommodate my needs by leading me into desperation. Similarly, one may need to experience the depths of depression in order to let go of attachments and become willing to take appropriate action. Once again, the Universe will accommodate.

While this "strong medicine" may seem cruel to some, I view this as the workings of a truly compassionate and supportive Universe. You set energy in motion toward a particular goal, and the Universe responds in a way that is uniquely appropriate to you. A dance with power ensues in which you are presented with opportunities to overcome your limitations and become more fulfilled.

Recognize and respect the power afoot in the Universe. Choose to operate in harmony with this energy in order to move toward completeness in-the-moment. Rely on your courage, daring, and "disciplined willingness," rather than desperation and despair, to follow the path of appropriate action.

I am not advocating "giving up" control to some outside source that might direct you to do terrible things. Remember, part of the seeker's discipline is to strengthen a view of the Universe that is secure, supportive and unified. Assume this is so and proceed—such a Universe will not direct you to do terrible things. As you develop clear mind, the fears of Thinking Mind are dropped. Since appropriate action springs from your commitment to be true to yourself and the situation, you will never become a slave to any ideology, dogma, or mystical power. You ride the invisible winds of the Universe and they carry you where you wish to go.

A woman I know contracted Leukemia and her health deteriorated steadily. She had always exhibited such vitality and joy that her condition seemed to be doubly pitiable. When her doctors began avoiding eye contact, she knew they had given up hope. One afternoon her father came to visit. As he prepared to leave, she asked, "Dad, what can I do?"

"Hang on, Honey, just hang on!" he replied, and left. About ten minutes later, by coincidence, her father-in-law, who was a minister, arrived to visit. Feeling weak and desperate, she pressed him with the same question, "Dad, what can I do?"

"Let go, Honey, let go," he said.

She took his advice and a sense of detachment and peace came to her. This feeling stayed with her as she got steadily worse. One day, during a visit from her minister, she slipped into a coma and was administered last rites. She was hooked to life support machines, but there was little hope. Twelve days later, hours before the machines were to be turned off, she woke and began to recover.

She said that during those days of coma, she had gone to a place suffused with white light where she was held and supported every moment, no matter which way she turned. She was without pain for the first time in many months. She is now healed and is once again a radiant presence. She was willing, when all seemed lost, to give up her resistance and accept her situation. In this state of acceptance, she experienced the support of the Universe in a very intimate and personal manner. Her newfound awareness has gained expression in her artistic work as well as her ability to be of service.

It is important to understand that by letting go, she did not give up. Rather she placed her trust in the appropriateness of the situation and assumed that whatever transpired would be for her highest good.

Receiving guidance is an interesting affair since the one being guided is an integral part of the process. Suppose you are enmeshed in a situation that is causing you great stress. You resolve to face this situation and are willing to do whatever it takes to bring about resolution, but you don't know what is required. You ask for guidance and then wait for a message. The Universe now sets about trying to send you instructions concerning the first step along the path to resolution. If your mind is exceptionally calm and clear, the communications may be very straightforward.

I had a bachelor friend who was ready to settle down but hadn't found the right woman. One evening he dozed off while reading a book. He woke up with a start and had the urgent feeling that he had to go to a particular singles bar right away. He was mystified since he didn't frequent such places, never drank alcohol, and didn't feel like going out. However, the feeling was strong enough that he got in his car and drove to the bar just to see what it was all about. He walked into the crowded night-spot and looked around. He saw a woman sitting with a group of friends and knew immediately that she was the reason he had come. They were married a short time later.

Most of us have not developed our intuitive abilities to the extent that my friend had, so this channel for direct communication of guidance is not often available. However, the Universe will keep trying to send the message in different ways until it is received, or you give up. The message may be contained in something a friend says, something you read, or hear on the radio. It often seems to come as an unusual opportunity to do something that leads you in a particular direction. How can you be sure you are receiving inspired guidance as opposed to hearing the whispering of "thinking mind?" You can't!

The warrior is alert for intuitive messages from within as well as from the world around him. Certain things appear as special messages and opportunities. He decides these are messages for him and acts on them with complete certainty, all of the time realizing these messages may be figments of his imagination. Since he has no expectations, he is never disappointed, and his trust in the Universe is never undermined. He has no regrets because he dwells in a world where mystery and beauty are his constant companions.

You cannot understand the mystery of the Universe, nor do you need to. As you are alert in the moment, the mystery of that moment is yours. Appropriate action is always available to you and you need only learn to listen in order for it to be revealed. If you leave fear behind, you can come into alignment with the flow of energy. In that moment, confusion disappears. If you act without confusion, internal conflict begins to lose its foothold.

It appears that as the world around us increases its already fevered pitch, more people are drawn to seek internal peace. They become warriors in the sense I have used this word, that is, they are resolved to experience fulfillment in their life. Some of them become impeccable warriors.

I had a conversation recently with a woman I hadn't seen

in about a year. I'll call her Laura. She is an attractive woman, about 35 years old, who has never been married. Laura has been seeking for meaning in her life for many years. She was previously a transient "house sitter" and had moved 32 times in six years. All of her belongings fitted into two large suitcases. She supported herself, but only worked sporadically, since she did not require much money.

Try as she might, she could not find the secret to inner peace. She didn't feel tied to any one place but longed to feel at home. She had found many men but never the right one.

One night she had a dream. In the dream, a young woman appeared and told her to travel by train to the East Coast, where she would find the home she had always wanted as well as a loving partner. She decided this dream contained the guidance she sought. Being an impeccable warrior, she made arrangements the next day to leave. Her friends held a gala going away party, and then she boarded the train with her two large suitcases. She left in high spirits and did not expect to ever return.

While on the train, she met someone from Boston who needed a house sitter for a few weeks. This led to other house sitting jobs which took her up and down the Atlantic Seaboard. Her life quickly took on the form of the life she thought she had left behind. She ended up, after several months, running a guest home in Maine, while the owners went south for winter vacation.

Her surroundings were desolate, and she seemed no closer to her goals than when she started. She became despondent and cried intermittently for several days. One night, just before the owners were to return, the young woman appeared again in her dreams. The woman instructed her to get on the train and go back to the place that she had left on the West Coast. There she would find what she was looking for!

When she woke, she was in a greater quandary than ever. She wondered what was going on. She considered the possibility that she was psychotic and should see a psychiatrist. It would certainly be simpler than all this traveling! However, her warrior's discipline prevailed. Upon the owners return, she took the money due her and bought the train ticket.

When she finally reached her destination and saw the familiar surroundings, the riddle was solved. She told me, "The home I was searching for was right here where I'd lived all these years. The person that I needed to love and make my life complete was myself." Resolution had occurred, and she was one step closer to completeness.

Let's step back for a moment and review what is being proposed. First of all, we can direct power with our thoughts and so can create, or draw to us, the events or things we visualize. This gives us a sense of power and control in our lives. While this seems much too good to be true (and certainly many won't believe it), it is , by itself, not terribly useful. We find that, as we follow the path of power, we really don't know what to "wish" for in order to resolve our internal conflicts. However, we don't have to worry about it. Help is available! All we have to do is ask and the path to resolution will be pointed out. We are guided to do certain things and power helps achieve them. One day resolution occurs.

If you had doubts about the notion of "power" as I have described it, then you must certainly believe I have wandered off to the "lunatic fringe of theory" with the concept of guidance. After all, if this is true, why doesn't everyone lead a serene and empowered existence? First of all, few people want to. Most of us are addicted to chaos and the stimulation of success, failure, buying, selling, winning, and losing. Internal turmoil is the norm and it is fine with us. "Doing" is what we are about and the "not doing" of clear mind is considered esoteric and impractical. The silence of meditation is practiced by a few oddballs but is certainly not mainstream.

Of course, many people overcome initial resistance and are willing to experiment with power. This is comfortable because getting more and having more is an important part of our culture. However, experimenting with guidance is another matter altogether. This requires that we act on "clues" and "intuitive messages." This is a risky business as we are stepping into the unknown. Few are willing to pursue this path relentlessly, but some are.

The warrior, in a sense, has no choice. She is committed to experiencing completeness in-the-moment and pursues this goal. At some point she discovers the warrior's discipline and begins to tighten up her life. As she begins to stand apart from chaos, her actions and thoughts become direct and powerful. Since her goal is completeness, the energy in the Universe is set in motion to move her in this direction. She is "guided" into situations where the learning that is required can take place. She senses this guidance and understands she must act on it in order to reach her goal. Since she leads an impeccable life in which she acts without expectation, but with total responsibility, fear does not stop her. Her existence becomes alive with mystery and joy, and she is complete.

THE WARRIOR'S DANCE

The energies of the world are in constant motion. We live in a dynamic world that is characterized by ebb and flow. The wind blows from the west and then from the east. The tide comes in and then goes out. People rise to prominence and fade to obscurity. Nations become world powers and then go into decline. No one can stop the tide and only a fool would try.

The warrior's challenge is to sense the flow of the energy around her and to move in harmony. Thus the flow carries her with little effort on her part and since she is never in opposition, her energy is not wasted. She knows the winds of the Universe blow in all directions, and that she needs only to ride one wind until it carries her to the next, in order to go where she chooses. Ultimately, riding the wind is the true joy and she cares little where it blows. This is what I call the warrior's "dance with power".

In a dance, one partner leads and the other follows. The

warrior's dance is more subtle in that sometimes he leads and sometimes he follows. His challenge is to know when to push and when to pull, when to walk and when to ride, when to go forward and when to retreat.

I have compared the warrior to a hawk on the wind. In order to soar, the hawk must leave his perch in the tree. The hawk knows the tree hides and protects him. The tree is known to him, but the world beyond the tree is unknown. The hawk in the tree becomes hungry. In order to eat, he must leave the tree and trust the wind to assist him in the hunt. If the hawk is cowardly, or obsessed with the comfort of the tree, he will starve. The image of a hawk that is afraid of leaving the tree to soar in the wind is a poignant one, because it speaks of unfulfilled promise. The warrior, like the hawk, cannot seek his goal from on high if he is not willing to surrender his fate to the wind.

The warrior knows that energy follows thought, and so focuses his thoughts. He holds highest the goal of experiencing completeness or fulfillment, however he knows this is a journey and not a destination. There are many intermediate stops along the way, and he calls upon power to help him move from one to the other. The warrior is always subject to the temptation of focusing his thoughts on what is known and comfortable, rather than "surrendering" to the winds of creation and letting them carry him effortlessly to his goal.

Irresistible energy is set in motion by the warrior who resolves to experience completeness. This energy carries him from one destination to the next on his journey toward his goal. He rests comfortably at each destination until the messenger comes to tell him it is time to be on the way. The warrior, being human, does not always want to leave the comfort of his stopping place. He may feel lazy, or fearful, or unprepared for the journey ahead. The warrior may be deluded into thinking he can use his mastery of power to resist resuming his journey, however this does not appear to be the case. Just as the hawk must leave the tree to hunt, so must the warrior leave the comfort of the warm hearth and surrender to the irresistible forces around him.

It is interesting that the warrior's choice to heed the messenger and continue her journey into the unknown is not truly a choice at all. We are all in the same boat, we must move into the unknown. If we don't go willingly, we will be dragged. Most people, given the same circumstances, will attempt to hang onto the known situation. We are like the little fellow who, on his first day at pre-school, clings to his mother's leg and won't let her go. He cries and suffers great mental anguish. After a while, he may notice all the other kids are playing and having a great time. If he is courageous, he will join them. Otherwise, his mother will give in and take him home. Unfortunately, he will have to face the same pain again on succeeding days until he can bring himself to let go and enjoy.

The fact that this process continues into adulthood is evidenced by all of the pain and fear we see around us. Many of us are indeed the "walking wounded." The warrior is not privileged. The difference is that, through discipline and courage, she chooses not to resist the forces around her. There is a very real reward for the master warrior. She may have pain, but she also has unreasonable joy. She dances the incredible dance with power that leads to completeness in the moment and suffering loses its meaning. When the messenger knocks, she greets him with joy and courage and follows where the messenger leads.

The warrior's "messenger" is, of course, internal anguish. I have spoken of this persistent messenger in the chapter "Beliefs." If we ignore his knock, he will knock louder. I have heard this knock many times myself and, on occasion, have had to be dragged kicking and screaming into the unknown.

For example, there was a time when my wife decided she could not live within the confines of our marriage, and was determined to leave. I ranted, raved, begged, and pleaded in an effort to change her mind, all to no avail. Our four year old daughter went with her. The situation was totally unacceptable to me. I kept trying to see her and bring her back by simply overpowering her with words and energy. Much to my chagrin, she was as determined to follow her own truth as I was to overcome it, and I could get no satisfaction. I sank into self-pity and decided I would welcome the end, secretly hoping my wife would feel sorry and guilty when I was gone.

In the midst of this turmoil, I turned forty. This event highlighted the injustice of the world. Not only was I alone, but I was alone and over forty! This seemed to be an unbearable and certainly undeserved indignity.

One morning about 6 AM, I woke up screaming. I lay thrashing on the bed with extreme pain in the pelvic area. After some time passed with no relief, it became obvious, that I needed help. I phoned my wife and asked her if she could take me to the Emergency Room. She said she would come as quickly as she could, and arrived a few minutes later with my daughter in tow. We immediately headed for the hospital. The pain was so severe that it was all I could do to stay in the car. When we arrived I was immediately put on a gurney to await the doctor's arrival. The nurse smiled down at me and said, "kidney stones."

Just what I needed. Now I was alone, over forty, and in the hospital with kidney stones. This was too much! This was not okay with me, and I let the Universe know it in no uncertain terms.

The doctor came and after confirming the nurse's suspicions, told me I would be in the hospital for a while. The pain subsided temporarily so my immediate discomfort was over. My wife had stayed to make sure I was all right, but needed to leave for work. She had tried to conduct herself in a manner that showed she was willing to help, but also made clear that this could in no way be used as a ploy to get her back. My attempts to hold her hand and elicit sympathy and guilt on her part were abortive.

I lay there alone, convinced I was one of the most unfairly treated "good" people around. Just then, the nurse walked in and said, "You are such a lucky man!" I looked at her with an unbelieving stare, my eyes as big as saucers. This woman had to be the most insensitive person on this part of the planet. However, anxious to preserve at least an appearance of dignity, I asked quietly, "Oh? Why do you say that?"

"You have such a lovely wife and daughter," she replied. She could not have said anything more deadly. It was like sticking a knife into me and then twisting it. The pain of losing my family engulfed me anew.

Suddenly, the lesson was clear. A grin began to spread slowly across my face. I had done it again. I had been trying to tell the world how to be, instead of embracing it as it was. How many times must I learn this lesson the hard way? I'm not here to criticize, I'm here to appreciate! I thanked the nurse for her kind words and she left. "Okay boys," I said, "you don't have to hit me again, I get the idea. I'm just here for the ride. Let's go!" I had a wonderful stay in the hospital.

Let's consider how the master warrior might have acted in my place when confronted with the situation I have just described. First of all, when faced with the pain of separation, he would just experience the pain. He would not judge it as good or bad but just "pain." Since he does not attach the pain to himself through judgment, after a while it leaves.

Now the warrior is alert because he knows the messenger has arrived and is beckoning to him. So how does he act towards his wife who is leaving? Is he calm and collected, perhaps a little aloof but loving? Maybe, but in this case he rants, raves, begs, and pleads, all to no avail! The difference is that he is not a victim and so does not lose his mastery. His actions are merely appropriate actions. Since he has dropped self image, there is no ego to be wounded. Without these wounds, there is no suffering and so no cause to be vindictive or seek revenge.

The situation is greeted as a learning experience, and his strength is not sapped by resistance. The warrior greets his fortieth birthday with the same sense of appreciation and wonder as all of the other days of his life. As he seeks and becomes completeness-in-this-moment, other moments past have no hold on him. Even kidney stones cannot unseat him from this moment. His focus is unwavering and his intent impeccable. He rides the turbulent energies with consummate skill and grace. He is the warrior, not the victim, and he has no regrets.

The anguish and suffering that I experienced when living through the situation described above, as well as other similarly traumatic periods, are in a large part responsible for my discovering the warrior's way. It became evident to me, as I grew older, that in some way I was continually repeating the same process. That is, a situation would arise that I viewed as being undesirable, unfair, or completely untenable. It could be the woman in my life wanted to leave me or, at times and just as bad, wanted to live with me. Maybe I had too much responsibility at work, or not enough. Whatever it was, I would judge a situation as "bad" and see myself as a victim with no hope of escape. I would begin to suffer intensely, all the time feeling sorry for myself. Being timid, I would let the situation get worse rather than dealing with it.

At some point I would become desperate. The desperation would overcome my fear and I would begin to act. Once motion was initiated, there was no turning back, and eventually I would come to resolution. The only problem with this process was that it was both painful and debilitating. The difference between my actions and those of the master warrior were that the warrior does not suffer mentally because he does not feel sorry for himself; the experience is not debilitating because he does not resist. As I grow older, I would hope to grow smarter. My attempt is to become the warrior.

This way of handling difficult situations probably sounds more idealistic than realistic, and one might even say that it sounds too good to be realizable. Could a real person be this master warrior, or am I just a naive Utopian thinker? Well, I ask you, what choices do I have? I could continue to suffer in my usual manner and gradually weaken as I grow older, or I can become the warrior! Is it impossible? Who knows? It is my challenge to find out.

Internal distress is, to the warrior, a signal that alerts her to the need for greater awareness. She prepares herself to receive intuitive instructions and follow them to resolution. In fact, she does this because she has no choice. She knows from experience that if she resists, the pain will get worse. As the warrior becomes proficient, internal anguish begins to subside. She no longer resists the flow of life and her body remains relaxed and fluid.

Her destiny is not, however, to be only a follower. A Zen monk told me that when he took formal vows to accept the precepts of Buddhism, he received the admonition, "Monk, here are your precepts. Know when to keep them and when to break them!" There are no inviolate rules to life. The warrior lives in a delicate balance with the forces of the Universe and must be prepared to lead as well as follow.

The warrior's dance takes on an infinite variety of forms in everyday life. For example, I had for many years dreamed of exploring the coastal waters of British Columbia and Alaska (the Inland Passage) by boat. I did not anticipate realizing this dream since I didn't know anything about boats, they cost lots of money, and I was basically afraid of the water.

Having grown up as an extremely cautious and somewhat timid person, I have had to develop a technique for dealing with "impossible" dreams. The first step is that I start telling people I am going to do a particular thing "someday." Then I start preparing to do it in small ways. After a while, the project develops an inertia and life of its own and it is very difficult to back out. This technique is, of course, just one method for putting into practice the "rules of power" that I have already discussed. That is, by "going public" with an idea, I am forced to focus on it. By being willing to take small steps in the required direction, the Universe has a means for providing me with the opportunities that will lead to eventual fulfillment of the goal.

In this case, I started by riding ferry boats in the both

British Columbia and Alaska. One day, at a friend's wedding reception, I met a fellow and his wife who fished commercially in Alaska. When I told them about my desire to take a small boat up the Inland Passage, they said they were going to make that trip in about two weeks, as they had to take their fishing boat, which was in Washington for repair work, to Alaska. We had all had enough champagne to be feeling quite jolly and sociable. They suggested I might like to make the trip with them. The next day, much to their surprise, and possibly consternation, I called and told them I was prepared to go along if they really wanted the company. The trip took about ten days, and we had a wonderful time.

I finally told some friends I would like to start looking for a small boat. We tossed our sleeping bags in the truck and spent several days in various fishing villages on the coast until we found the boat we were looking for. My friends made the deal, and I wrote a check for Precious. I was absolutely paralyzed with fear at what I had done. My friends drove while I sat in a catatonic state, much to their amusement. My terror was multi-faceted. I felt guilty about spending money frivolously when I had a family to support, I had no idea how to maintain and operate a boat, and I was still afraid of the water!

It was a few weeks before I had recovered sufficiently to even see the boat. I hired a boat-hauler to transport it the 150 miles to my house. Precious was a small commercial fishing vessel that had been built in the 1920's and was in need of considerable work. I spent the next two and a half years rebuilding it. By the time I was done, I knew the boat pretty well.

After the launching I used the boat frequently, but it quickly became obvious that I needed a bigger boat for family cruising. The Precious had spartan accommodations for two fisherman, but I needed accommodations for five or six people–the family and one or two experienced friends to help run the boat (remember, I was still afraid of the water). I don't know how I failed to notice that the boat was so small. Maybe I knew that if I didn't start small, I wouldn't start at all.

My intuitive feeling was that it was time for me to consider getting the larger boat, even though the present one had only been in the water for a short time. My wife encouraged me to follow my inner voice. I made the decision that I would buy a larger boat if it became possible.

The first problem was I didn't have the money. A few weeks later my boss called me into his office and said I was to be one of the recipients of an annual cash award given by the company for outstanding technical contribution! This, combined with the sale of my old boat, would give me the money I needed. It occurred to me, when I received the award, that there were much more responsible uses for the money than to satisfy my maritime fantasies. It made the most sense to save the money for my daughter's college education. However, I also understood that I had called upon the Universe to help me to buy a boat and it had responded. The ball was in my court. I decided, with my wife's concurrence, to press ahead.

I started looking for boats, but they were either unsatisfactory or out of my price range. I began asking in meditation for the "right boat at the right price" to be provided. One day as I was taking a walk by the local marina, I saw a boat arrive that was of the type I was looking for. I went down to the dock and struck up a conversation with the owner. When I mentioned I was looking for a similar boat, he said that he had been thinking of selling his. The price he quoted was very reasonable and the boat seemed to be just right for my needs. I ended up buying the boat after a careful survey.

Unfortunately, I hadn't sold my other boat yet and summer had ended. Every one told me there was no hope of selling it until spring. I needed the money for the new boat, but the situation was not promising. There was no response to a classified add I placed in the newspaper. Once again, I decided to employ visualizations. I began to visualize my boat being sold to a happy buyer. I only had a few days left in which to sell the boat before I left on a business trip that was to last several weeks. It looked like the boat would have to remain in the marina for the winter. The day before I left I received a phone call from a man who said he noticed the "For Sale" sign on my boat. He wondered if he could go aboard and look it over. I arranged to meet him and we went for a short boat ride. He bought the boat that evening.

We made our first trip into British Columbia the next summer. A couple that had fished commercially for many years came with us to help run the boat. We had a wonderful time cruising and fishing. The "impossible dream" had become a reality.

I describe these events to show you how subtle the dance with power can be. On the surface, nothing very unusual is happening and yet all of the doors open at the appropriate time so you can get where you are going. It looks to others as though you achieve your goals through perseverance and luck. You, on the other hand, see the invisible miracle in each coincidence that brings you closer to your goal. Further, you perceive that the goal itself was pointed out to you as being appropriate to experiencing the fulfilled life.

If you are sensitive to the balance between choice, discipline, power, and guidance, you proceed along the path with no resistance. As you become experienced, you see worry is not only futile, but unnecessary. You proceed with confidence, and the boundaries begin to blur. You are no longer sure whether you are choosing or following directions. Coincidences become miracles, and miracles become coincidences. Miraculous power blends with physical effort to produce the ordinary. The ordinary is magic and miraculous in the highest degree. You are dancing with power.

Life is a continued experience of broadening awareness. I am overwhelmed by the miracle of it and embrace the process with my whole heart. I appreciate the opportunity to be a witness and give thanks that it is so. The internal suffering however, I recognize as my own. It is just me dragging my feet on the path, when I should be stepping lightly along. For me there is no choice but to seek the warrior's way and to engage in his dance.

≈ 28 ≈

FINDING
WITHOUT
SEEKING

Let's assume this book has come to you at just the right time. There was something stirring inside that wanted to reach for more light in your life but didn't know where to look. The voice from this book has struck up a rapport with your own inner voice and you are determined to move higher. You still don't know where to go, but you hope you will be "guided" in the right direction.

You have started to introduce discipline into your life and have even tried meditating. Not much has come of it, but you haven't quit entirely. Your resolve to go forward is strong, but you can see that old habits are also strong, and you are not sure which is going to prevail. At times you think your efforts are being reaffirmed by "miraculous coincidences" but just as often you believe you are sinking into a deep pit from which there is no real escape.

Let me offer a few comments. First of all, once you set energy in motion along the path to greater awareness, you don't have to really do much except go for the ride because it is almost impossible to stop. Usually, the motion towards awareness is like a roller coaster ride with lots of peaks and dips before it smoothes out. Unlike a roller coaster, it is sometimes difficult to see the motion at all. Don't worry; all of the time that you are saying, "It's not working", it is. You can drag your feet and slow things down but it's very hard to stop. Remember, in the end, you are only looking for what you already have, this moment of awareness. The only difference will be how much you appreciate it.

If you sense you are losing your focus, reread this book or find another one that leaps off the bookstore shelf at you. Remember, your truth is within you. All a "self-help" book can do is help you to listen to it. Be quick to recognize and express appreciation for any insights or "coincidences" that you perceive as assistance from the Universe. Don't worry about "being the fool" by thanking some power that may not even exist. In fact, the Universe doesn't need your thanks. This is just a mechanism for developing the attitude that we live in a supportive Universe. This is one of the "tricks" for strengthening resolve, and developing courage and daring. I suggest that you don't question it; just do it. You have nothing to lose.

A period of doubt after initial enthusiasm is not uncommon. I encourage you to maintain your discipline and not be overcome by doubts.

You are now ready to use the technique of becoming a "living koan". To do this, first decide what your most pressing problem or greatest ambition is. Remember, internal unrest is the messenger who has come to tell you it is time to move toward greater awareness. That is, find the one thing in your life that you most desperately desire to have resolved. Whatever it is, affirm to yourself that you are ready to seek resolution for this pressing problem or ambition and call on Guidance and Power to assist you. Be prepared, this is not a joke! Or, conversely, this may be a joke, and it may take a while for you to see the humor in it. In either case, you have set energy in motion towards resolution.

For the sake of discussion, let's say you have focused on your most pressing problem. It is advantageous for you, at this point, to accept your present circumstances without rancor. Understand that the situation you find yourself in has given you valuable understanding and insight. It is as good a place as any from which to seek resolution. For example, if you perceive your problem is that you don't have enough money, accept this as a great opportunity to learn about financial well being. Once again, embrace each situation that presents itself, accept the challenge offered by the situation, and never consider yourself a victim.

Now you are ready to proceed with your life as usual, but something is different. You are looking for clues. They will start to present themselves to you in very short order, but you must be alert or you will miss them. Once a clue is perceived, you have to decide whether or not to act on it. Listen to your intuition!

I once felt I wanted more free time but needed to work to support my family. This was a problem for me and I decided to deal with it, although it seemed impossible to resolve. Within a few hours, I ran into an acquaintance that I hadn't seen in a couple of years. When I asked him what he had been doing since I saw him last, he replied, "Whatever I choose." This sounded intriguing, and I suggested we have a cup of coffee at the local cafe, if he could spare the time. He said he had as much time as I needed as the Universe supported him, and in return he gave his time to people like me. It was obvious to me that I was supposed to talk to this man.

During our ensuing conversation, I mentioned that earning the money I wanted was a dilemma for me. He said there were always ways to make money and suggested investing $2000 in a particular highly speculative venture. This sounded like a "clue" to me, and I wondered if I should participate. A friend, who had joined us at the table, said, "Hey, I'll do that!" I wrestled with my feelings for a few minutes and decided against it. It just didn't "feel" right to me, even though there was little doubt in my mind about the success of the venture. My friend invested the money and made several thousand dollars in a few months.

Meanwhile, this fellow suggested I read a particular book. This was the clue I was looking for. The book pointed me in the direction I needed to travel. I have never had any regret about choosing the clue that said "read this book" over receiving several thousand dollars. I'm just following instructions.

As you act upon clues, new insight and energy come into your life. You find you are attracting the most improbable coincidences, and they support you in your search. You may find that other problems resolve themselves along the way.

I am sure you can appreciate, at this point, the importance of the warrior's discipline. First, one must have access to Silent Mind in order to perceive clues to appropriate action. This implies letting go of chaos in your life and bringing Thinking Mind under control—meditation is one approach. Mental and physical disciplines help to strengthen the attributes of courage and daring, which are required if one is to follow the inner voice.

Another way to state the warrior's challenge is—live without resistance. Dropping judgment and self-image are the stepping stones to accomplishing this. While this may sound like a totally ridiculous concept, it is amazing how free you feel once you get the hang of it. We are very attached to our personalities and opinions and don't believe that we, or the world, can get along without them. You might even think life would be drab and uninteresting without judgment and self-image. In my opinion, nothing could be farther from the truth. As you quit judging, you quit resisting. Life becomes a journey of action and appreciation of the moment. Your energy is no longer sapped by the struggle to resist change and deal with a world that is "all wrong."

A close friend spent several years building a house that he and his family occupied. It was a modest but comfortable house, beautifully situated on a bluff looking out over the water. There were plenty of trees around the house along with a wonderful garden. He liked the house very much and was proud of his handiwork. The house was on the edge of town which occasioned considerable "chauffeuring" of the kids on his wife's part. Another difficulty was that the house only had two bedrooms and his daughter was at the point where she needed more privacy than sharing a room with her brother afforded. He felt this was a minor problem since there was a large daylight basement that he could finish off for additional living space as soon as he had some spare time.

One day his wife suggested that, for these and other reasons, they consider moving into town. He couldn't believe that she would suggest such a course of action.

The house was part of his identity and, in many ways, told the world who he was. When people first came to the house, the knotty pine walls and American Indian beadwork that they displayed made a statement about the inhabitants and their way of life. The setting was serene and the view spectacular. Further, the thought of moving all of his woodworking machinery was enough to deter him from ever wanting to move again. He had hoped to grow old improving the place a little at a time. He asked his wife for some time to consider the matter.

After three days he told her that he couldn't even consider moving. The very thought caused great inner turmoil; he was losing sleep and becoming irritable. He asked his wife to drop the subject. He didn't feel good about this, but was relieved when she said she would. He understood that nothing had really been resolved but was hoping to "let sleeping dogs lie."

About six months later, she said unexpectedly, "I still think we ought to move." Her husband's reply was, "No problem!" They bought the first house they looked at two days later. His willingness to move was as much a surprise to him as it was to his wife. He felt his wife was justified in wishing to move, and he was happy that he could now comply. He told me he was very much relieved that his resistance to moving had disappeared. It occurred to him that life was much easier and more fun without this resistance.

One might say that the Universe is trying to respond to your desires as expressed by the thoughts and attitudes you hold. If you hold a vision of a fulfilled life, the Universe will attempt to lead you in the direction of fulfillment. All you have to do is put aside the resistance engendered by fear and judgment and move toward resolution.

Maybe you have had the experience of having a five year old "help" you bake her birthday cake. In this case, the child wants the cake and you want her to have it. Depending on the child, the process can be relatively efficient or painfully slow. Children often want to do things that are beyond their motor skill capabilities and knowledge. On the one hand, you want to accommodate the child because it is a learning process, while on the other hand you know that some operations are tedious at best or doomed to outright failure unless you help out. In some cases, the child may even snatch the measuring cup out of your hand and insist on deciding how much of each ingredient to use without your interference.

Our personal situation is like that of the child doing the baking. If you choose to experience resolution, the Universe moves to accommodate. However, you may need to grow in awareness to achieve your goal. As the Universe moves to deliver these lessons, you may be like the little child that resists directions and keeps trying to be in charge.

For example, suppose that in order to experience true peace, you must learn, among other things, that material goods do not equate to happiness. An opportunity to learn this lesson is provided by losing your job. As your economic situation begins to become tenuous, you try to cling to the things you own. You begin to do affirmations for more money and feel victimized. Panic begins to set in and you are farther from internal peace than ever. At some point you may become desperate and let go. You can now learn your lesson.

Consider a different approach. Suppose you refrain from judging the loss of your job as "bad." You know the messenger has knocked and it is time to move toward greater awareness. You do not see yourself as a victim but a warrior following the directions of Silent Mind in order to reach your desired goal. You replace fear with trust and move forward without resistance. How do you know this makes sense? You don't–but you choose to operate this way because the alternative is to be the victim and live in fear and self-pity. Your life is a living experiment.

As your life becomes the impeccable life of the warrior, you begin to feel power and experience the Universe affirming your desire to bring light into your life. Trust and confidence grow and gradually become part of you. Your discipline focuses on this feeling of trust and you proceed courageously. However, we are still human. At times, we see the impossibility of it all. Our courage slips from us and we are exposed for what we are; frightened and alone we stand naked before the immensity of the unknown power that surrounds us. All of our discipline is seen as an attempt to hide from our true situation, which appears to be hopeless. It was at such a time, I believe, that Christ on the cross called out, "Father, why hast thou forsaken me?" He was not blaming a father in heaven, but was in despair that he could not find courage and trust within himself at that moment. This happens to each of us again and again. Our courage deserts us and we feel abandoned. Deep inside, we know we have been moving in harmony with the energy around us, and yet, at that moment, we feel devoid of inner strength.

At times such as these, depend on your discipline to carry you through. Thinking Mind has been quietly waiting for you to lower your guard and become complacent. It has waited for your focus to waiver ever so slightly and then seized the opportunity. When you least expect it, Thinking Mind has come to the fore with its view of separation, and shattered the unity perceived by Silent

Mind. If you panic, Thinking Mind has won; if you proceed thoughtfully and with discipline, Thinking Mind will slowly relinquish its strangle hold and balance will be restored.

It appears that to gain new understanding, we have to be willing to continually let go of the old. The warrior's life is characterized by this feeling of continual rebirth and motion without resistance. This translates to a feeling of freedom and, without the burden of judgment, lightness. These are elements of "unreasonable joy".

Another part of the path toward transformation that seems to be consistent is service to others. President Kennedy said, "Ask not what your country can do for you, but what you can do for your country." I don't know if he wrote this line, but when he uttered it many people were set on the path toward greater awareness. Many people were moved, for the first time in a long time, to engage in humanitarian service with very little economic reward, most notably through the Peace Corps. I have no idea if this helped the Third World countries, but I do know that the volunteers I have met all said they gained at least as much from the service as they were able to give. This seems to be a common attitude among those that have given freely of themselves in order to be of assistance to others.

We all have the opportunity to act from different vantage points in our daily lives. The most prevalent point-of-view is probably that we are victims of our fate. Hard work may help, but it certainly does not guarantee a fulfilling life. You are either lucky or unlucky in your endeavors and there is not much you can do about it. In other words, "Life is hard and then you die."

A second view is the self-centered approach to the world. In this case, you accept responsibility for your own circumstances and set out to satisfy your desires and needs. This is a responsible approach to life which leads to at least temporary gratification as you meet each of your own needs. Little energy is wasted complaining about your circumstances, since you feel in charge and reject the role of victim.

In this scheme of things, however, your self interest must, at some time, take precedence over that of others and your joy is often, in some way, at the expense of another's pain. This approach is characterized by a supply that never meets the demand. It seems that there is never enough to "go around", and while some experience abundance, others experience lack. This seems to be the way of the world with little one can do about it. Many ride this roller coaster of pleasure and pain to their death, trying, but seldom succeeding, in achieving a sense of true fulfillment.

The spiritual warrior's way is different. You recognize that you are powerful and the external world is a mirror for your beliefs and attitudes. You are determined to share in your divine birthright and experience the joy of being complete and without need. You realize that any attempt to satisfy your own needs first is a reflection of the belief that you are indeed needy. In order to avoid this trap, you take the following course of action: you declare, "I am complete and trust that all of my needs will be met. Since I have nothing pending, how may I best show appreciation for the gift of life?" Now you proceed as though you believe it.

As you see opportunities to demonstrate appreciation and act on them, you begin the journey toward becoming that which you have affirmed yourself to be. These opportunities often present themselves as situations in which you may be of service.

As you act from confidence rather than need, you find your experience matches your assumptions. That is, the abundance that flows through you also sustains you, and so your needs are met. You find you can give without taking and bring joy without pain–therefore you feel complete. You begin the dance of unity in which you recognize the spirit in all things, including yourself.

It is important to recognize that the warrior is no martyr who puts others needs before her own. She assumes that her needs are already met. That is, she puts no one's needs before her own because she assumes that she is without need! Further, she assumes that each person is responsible for their own circumstance, and she is under no obligation to anyone. Her only concern is to experience her lack of need. And so she asks, "How may I be of service?" and proceeds to do whatever comes to mind. In this case, there is no one to save because there is no victim. There is no obligation because there is no need to be of service. The act of service is just a dance of celebration in a Universe that is already complete.

I have a friend, Steve, who is a construction worker in New York City. He had a difficult childhood and, being of Puerto Rican descent, experienced considerable discrimination in his life. As a teenager, he was involved in full scale gang wars between hundreds of young toughs. Weapons of choice were baseball bats, chains, bricks, and occasionally a zip gun made from a car antenna. He grew into adulthood as an alcoholic and drug user. His powerful build helped to hide the fact that he was a mass of fear and insecurity. He carried an Italian Berretta (pistol) in a shoulder holster for protection on the streets. He had never killed anyone, but was no stranger to violence.

He married while in his thirties, but the otherwise good relationship could not survive his mounting alcohol and drug problems. His life lacked meaning and direction; he was lonely and his prospects did not look good.

Steve worked as a mason doing repair work on old brick buildings. He was not allowed into the union for many years because of his Puerto Rican heritage. Finally, his wife convinced him to stand up to the union leaders and warn them that if he weren't admitted, he would stage a sit-in. They admitted him immediately, and he rose to a position of authority in the union local.

One night, Steve noticed a woman at a meeting in the union hall. She was the only woman present and looked somewhat out of place among the rough construction workers. He recognized her as the daughter of one of the union officials. They had met but never talked before. He knew she worked as a mechanic erecting scaffolding, which was a very unusual job for a woman at that time. He thought that she must be an interesting person and decided to get to know her better.

In the course of the conversation that followed, he found out she was starting training to do volunteer hospice work at a nearby hospital. She suggested that Steve might like to become involved also. He was somewhat shocked at the idea of working with the dying. Many of the patients had AIDS, which was a terrifying prospect. To work with these patients and not even get paid for it was almost incomprehensible.

Nevertheless, Steve became a volunteer. Immediately, his life began to change. He began to feel a power in his life that was never there before, and occasionally a sense of joy would bubble up with no reason.

His job of repairing masonry on old building fronts required that he work on scaffolding, sometimes as much as sixty stories high. He had been doing it for many years, but he had a growing fear of climbing out onto the scaffolding. He always carried a flask of whiskey on the job and used it to keep the fear at bay. This, he told me, was not unusual; most of the men did it.

Meanwhile, the hospice work was giving him a new kind of courage. By helping people in the process of dying, he was sharing in a most profound experience. As he did this, he let down his own barriers and was no longer afraid to be perceived as soft and loving. One evening, he confessed his hidden fear of heights to his friend Gloria. "Steve," she told him, "look for the fear inside." He wasn't quite sure what to make of this but understood that what she had said was important.

He continued work in his usual manner. One day he was sent to help repair a walkway that went between two buildings thirty stories in the air. He was to work from pipe scaffolding, which meant climbing all the way from street level. As he passed the seventeenth floor, the thought struck him that he hadn't been drinking. Then a greater realization swept over him—he wasn't afraid. The marvel of it was so overwhelming that he abandoned the ladder and began climbing around on the outside of the scaffolding shouting, "Thank you, Gloria! Thank you, Gloria!"

The boss, who was above him, thought he was in trouble and began calling to him to find out what the problem was. He was rather mystified when Steve, with a big grin, assured him nothing was wrong.

Steve had met and conquered what Don Juan (Carlos Casteneda) calls man's first natural enemy: fear. How did this happen? Steve, through his intimate relationship with many dying people in the hospice program, had felt love transcend the physical boundaries of the body and, eventually, the boundary between life and death. He had truly experienced the unity of the Universe through caring. As this happened, he lost his fear of death at the deepest level. Once he had lost fear of the ultimate unknown–death–he weakened the foundation upon which fear is built, and it was only a matter of time before the whole structure collapsed. It is interesting that in the processes, a shiny new structure was built; that of trust.

As Steve continues to give more of himself through his hospice work, his life becomes increasingly more powerful and exciting. He had the experience a few years ago of having a hundred pound piece of terra cotta drop on his foot. When it happened, he summoned the power within him and shouted, "This is beautiful! I love it!" As men came to help him, he continued to say this. He was taken to the hospital where they removed his shoe, which was full of blood, and they found that three of his toes were broken. He never felt any pain, then or later. Men are often hurt doing this type of work, and Steve has had several similar, although not so serious, injuries since. His body bleeds, bruises, and swells, but he continues to not feel pain.

This event is deeply significant for all of us because it points a direction and holds out a promise. Steve has met the warrior's ultimate challenge to drop self pity and never be a victim. Rather, he is so filled with appreciation for the gift of life that he even embraced the moment in which his foot was crushed by a heavy piece of masonry.

This is indeed a lofty example for all of us, but why no pain? Steve told me that in his hospice work he had discovered that much of the physical pain patients experience is attached to emotional pain they carry within them.

One woman, whose son was an alcoholic, was dying of cancer. She was experiencing great physical pain and, in addition, carried the guilt and emotional pain of her son's alcoholism. Steve suggested that it was late in her life to be harboring the intense emotional distress associated with her son's addiction, and she should replace it with love and trust. The woman was able to do this, and as the emotional pain subsided, her physical pain lessened greatly and became bearable.

Steve began to apply the lesson in his own life. He let go of his judgments and let his life be guided by love and trust. When the masonry fell on his foot, he did not judge the event as "bad." At the exact moment when most of us would be cursing the Universe that spawned such an event, he yelled, "This is beautiful! I love it!" Instead of attaching emotional pain to the event, he attached love and exhilaration. Thus physical pain had nothing to cling to and could not gain a foothold.

Does this mean that someone who has transcended the emotional pain of judgment and self-pity will always be free of physical pain? I don't think so. My understanding is that this is experienced differently by different people. However, without the emotional pain, the physical pain becomes just an experience; it does not become the master. In this sense you are "free" of pain because, while you may experience it, it is an experience equal to all of your other experiences and cannot obsess and enslave you.

Steve said he is sometimes able to relieve the pain of others. He has, on several occasions recently, had patients tell him that their pain went away when he touched them with his hands. On other occasions he has been "guided" to do visualizations with patients in order to relieve their suffering. This technique has also been very successful. When asked what "guides" him, Steve says he doesn't know. He commented, "I don't know about God or if there is one. My religion is whatever my patient needs it to be in order to bring solace. I will pray as a Catholic, a Jew, a Moslem, or whatever else is required to bring peace."

I have saved Steve's story for this chapter because he provides us with a clear example of someone whose life is a continual process of transformation. The more he embraces life, the more "unreasonable joy" pervades it. Steve's mechanism for transformation has been hospice work, however he is an impeccable "warrior." This is reflected in his attitude, his diet, and his physical discipline.

On his sixtieth birthday, he told me he loved his life more than ever before and he didn't wish to be a day younger. He said that all of the pain of his younger life, and a hundred times more, would be worth it to be where he is today. This is finding without seeking.

ABOUT THE AUTHOR

The author holds a Ph. D. in Electrical
Engineering and was Vice President and
Chief Engineer of Stanford Telecommuni-
cations Inc., a Silicon Valley electronics
company, until its sale in 1999. He has
authored a number of technical papers
and holds 15 patents related to spread
spectrum communications. He currently
facilitates workshops that emphasize
movement, creativity, and self-discovery.
This is his first book.

You may contact the author via email at:
natnatali@yahoo.com